The TRAD Guide to Joshua Tree

60 FAVORITE Climbs from 5.5 to 5.9

By Charlie and Diane Winger

Published by The Colorado Mountain Club Press. Founded in 1912 the Colorado Mountain Club is the largest outdoor recreation, education and conservation organization in the Rocky Mountains. Look for our books at your favorite book seller or contact us at:

710 10th Street, Suite 200, Golden, CO 80401
Phone (303) 996-2743, Email address: hanisg@cmc.org
Website: http://www.cmc.org

Managing Editor for CMC Press: Gretchen Hanisch.
Graphics Design and Maps: Andrew Terrill and Gretchen Hanisch.
Proofing: Peg Quinn, Gretchen Hanisch and Andrew Terrill.
All photographs in this book by Charlie and Diane Winger, except as credited.
Front cover photo: Diane and Charlie Winger.
Front cover design: Terry Root.
Back cover photo: Diane and Charlie Winger.
Text copyright 2004: Charlie and Diane Winger.

The Trad Guide to Joshua Tree
by Charlie and Diane Winger

Library of Congress Control Number: 2004112095
ISBN #0-9724413-9-5

We gratefully acknowledge the financial support of the people of Colorado through the Scientific and Cultural Facilities District of greater metropolitan Denver, for our publishing activities.

SCFD
Scientific & Cultural
Facilities District
Making It Possible.

Printed in Canada

ACKNOWLEDGEMENTS

We have shared many fun-filled days, and more than just a few beers at Joshua Tree over the years with a multitude of friends. They have all contributed in some manner or other to the writing of this Guide. We have listed their names here so you will recognize them as the sandbaggers and bottom feeders they are, people who would trick you into climbing some horror story of a route and then say, "you really didn't climb *that* route?"

For Dave ("Perro Grande") Cooper, Steve Dodson, Jim Foley, Ginni ("the GinMaster") Greer, Jerry Harder, Steve and Shane Holonitch, Gary Hoover, Tom ("Snake-man") Maceyka, Meredith ("Rope Gun") Lazaroff, Alan ("Our Mentor") Mosiman, Randy ("Rock Legend" - or is that an "Illusion") Murphy, Dave ("Remedial") Reeder, Patrice Steinke, and, last but not least, the biggest sandbagger of them all, Veikko ("trust me, it'll go") Kammonen. We look forward to the day when you will pull just a little bit harder on that top rope so we can make that one move that's just out of our reach! Hopefully, we've not forgotten someone who will later return to tie knots in the middle of our climbing rope while we're sleeping!

We wouldn't trade any of them for an IRS audit! We hope that we will share many, many more memorable days in the sun with <u>you</u> on the sharp end of the rope. Have fun and climb safely.

We'd also like to express our thanks to Alison Conrad, Ginni Greer, Dave Cooper, and Meredith Lazaroff for being our guinea pigs and critiquing all our approach and route descriptions. Sorry about those times we tried to send you off a cliff or into a yucca!

A special acknowledgement to all of the pioneer climbers at Joshua Tree, and especially to Rangy Vogel and Alan Bartlett, whom we've never had the pleasure of meeting, for all of their outstanding original route research. Their excellent guidebooks have provided us with many hours of climbing enjoyment.

Alan Mosiman has been a true Climbing Mentor, great climbing partner, and good friend to both of us for many years.

TABLE OF CONTENTS

Climb grades: 5.5/5.6   5.7   5.8   5.9

The authors' favorite climbs:

JOSHUA TREE

PREFACE

Climbing magazines always seem to have numerous articles about someone "sending" a 5.14d or other such high end route. We're not that talented. The only thing we've ever "sent" was a check to the IRS to pay our taxes. Well, we want to "send" you to Joshua Tree National Park for some fun rock climbing adventures in the sun.

We think climbing is relative (except our relatives won't climb with us!). Your first 5.7 or 5.8 is just as challenging and exciting to you as those bigger numbers are to the climber on the cover of a climbing magazine.

In planning this Guide, we have compiled a collection of our favorite beginning and intermediate routes. We've had the most fun climbing these; no run-out psycho stuff, just plain, good, old fashioned traditional ("Trad") climbing. Remember, beauty is in the eye of the beholder! Having said that, you may have guessed that this Guide does not contain any pure "sport" routes - those that don't involve placing protection, your basic "dip and clip" scenario.

We have arranged the routes on a geographical basis to stress minimal approach times and a maximum amount of climbing time. The notable exception is Mental Physics, which has about a 1 hour approach. Yet, what would a visit to the Park be if you allowed this gem to remain unclimbed?

But, just so you won't forget how to do Sport Routes, we've occasionally thrown in a route which contains a "token" bolt. We've always been happy to see the bolt that protects those final moves on Overhang Bypass after the traverse.

Lest you think we're anti-Sport Route, let it be said that Joshua Tree has some of the finest sport routes in the country - some that we've climbed many, many times. One climb in particular stands out in our memories. Every evening before dinner we would make a "final run" at the SW Corner route on the Headstone, located near Ryan Campground, and it always continued to be an adventure.

In addition to the climbs presented in this Guide, there are a multitude of other climbing possibilities in Joshua Tree. We've heard that there are on the order of 5,000 named routes in Park. These routes include everything from the multi-starred 5.3, The Eye, to unbelievable 5.14+ routes.

Some of the routes in this Guide will challenge you, some of them you could do in your sleep, but you'll always be assured of having a good time climbing them and socializing afterwards with your friends. There's nothing like a good day of climbing followed by a couple of cool cervezas with our friends. It never failed to amaze (or amuse) us just how enthralled we all were when someone explained (with animation) the moves they made "sending" that death-defying 5.7 roof problem.

As with all climbing endeavors, we advocate the use of helmets, ropes and other safety gear. Remember, there is always a tomorrow; make sure you are around to enjoy it. There's nothing macho about taking a "grounder" and becoming paralyzed or paying the ultimate price - being dead. Climb safely, climb courteously, and climb responsibly.

We sincerely hope that you will enjoy climbing these routes time and time again, much as we have. Remember, rock climbing is fun!

Overhang Bypass

JOSHUA TREE

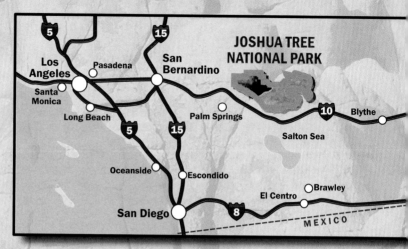

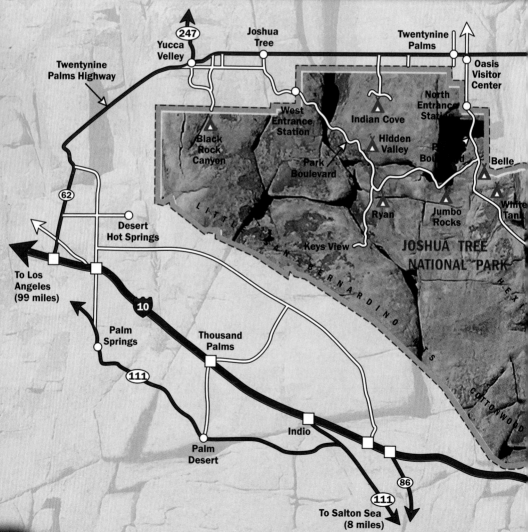

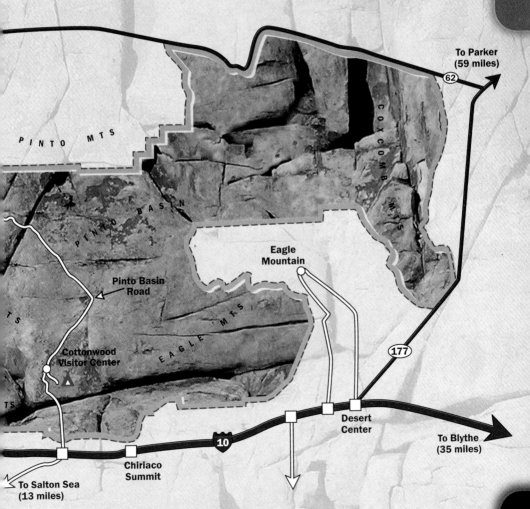

JOSHUA TREE NATIONAL PARK

Main map scale (in miles)

0   5   10   15

JOSHUA TREE

To Parker
(59 miles)

62

PINTO MTS

COXCOMB MTS

PINTO BASIN

Eagle
Mountain

Pinto Basin
Road

177

EAGLE MTS

Cottonwood
Visitor Center

Desert
Center

To Blythe
(35 miles)

10

Chiriaco
Summit

To Salton Sea
(13 miles)

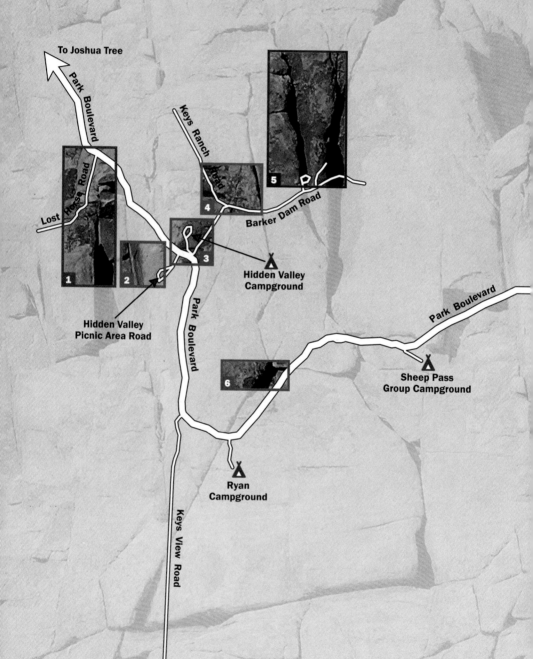

To Joshua Tree

Park Boulevard

Keys Ranch Road

Lost Horse Road

Barker Dam Road

Hidden Valley
Campground

Hidden Valley
Picnic Area Road

Park Boulevard

Park Boulevard

Sheep Pass
Group Campground

Keys View Road

Ryan
Campground

1
2
3
4
5
6

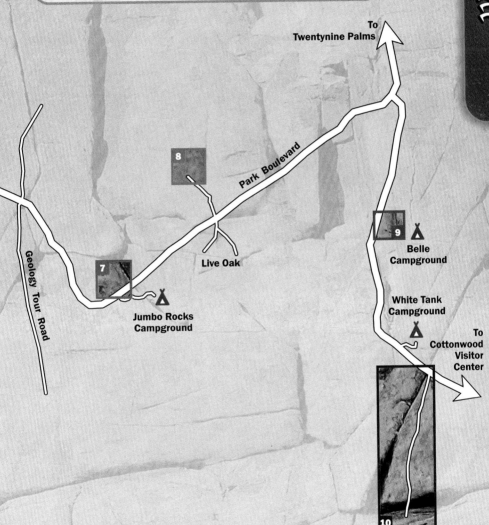

JOSHUA TREE CLIMBING AREAS

1 Lost Horse Area
2 Real Hidden Valley
3 Hidden Valley Campground Area
4 Echo Rock Area
5 Wonderland of Rocks

6 Sheep Pass Area
7 Jumbo Rocks
8 Split Rocks
9 Belle Campground Area
10 White Tank - Stirrup Tank Area

0   1   2
Scale (in miles)

JOSHUA TREE

To
Twentynine Palms

Park Boulevard

8

Live Oak

9
Belle
Campground

White Tank
Campground

To
Cottonwood
Visitor
Center

7

Geology Tour Road

Jumbo Rocks
Campground

10

Climber getting to grips with Toe Jam

iNTRODUCTION

Joshua Tree National Park: a unique place of 5,000 quality climbing routes situated within two desert ecosystems. The western portion of the Park lies within the Mojave Desert, which has an elevation around 3,000 feet (914m) and above. The Colorado Desert occupies the eastern portion of the Park at elevations generally below 3,000 feet.

The Mojave Desert, being higher, is generally cooler and receives more precipitation than does its next door neighbor, the Colorado. The Mojave Desert area is commonly referred to as the "high desert" while the Colorado is known as the "low desert".

There is no "line in the sand" dividing these two deserts, but there are some easily identifiable plant and temperature differences. All of those Joshua Trees which grow so abundantly higher up are conspicuously absent from the lower, hotter, and drier desert out toward Cottonwood campground. Incidentally, those plants we refer to as Joshua Trees really aren't "trees". They have no rings as do normal trees; they're actually giant Yucca plants. Photographs have been used to determine their age and rate of growth.

It's worth the drive to head past White Tank and Belle campgrounds to view Pinto Basin. While on your way to explore this Colorado Desert area, stop and experience "Where Two Deserts Meet", a short, fun, 5.8 climb located near the parking area at the intersection of Pinto Basin Road and the Stirrup Tank turnoff.

There is a wide diversity of plant and animal life to view while you're running around ticking off all of these exciting climbs. Some of these you'll see, some you'll hear and some are so quick you'll wonder if you really saw them and the others, well, some folks would just as soon not have had the experience.

Joshua Trees dominate the landscape in the "high" desert, but hidden below these sometimes towering sentinels are the iron-like creosote bushes, a wide variety of wildflowers and cactus that bloom in the spring. Creosote bushes have a particularly pungent smell and were very useful to the native desert dwellers as medicines.

As you proceed lower in the Park toward Cottonwood campground, you'll encounter the beautiful and always-popular Cholla Cactus Gardens; not a place you would want to consider running through in your birthday suit! That's painful even to think about. The Cholla Cactus is commonly referred to as the "jumping cactus". You won't be "jumping" with joy if one of them attaches itself to your bare skin. Hint: a comb with big teeth works well to remove the cactus; anything else will likely result in memorable pain.

Charlie Winger on lead

Moonrise over Joshua Tree

A little further down the road another attraction to visit is the Ocotillo Patch. The Ocotillo is a tall, willowy plant that produces beautiful red blooms mainly in the spring after a rain. You're in the Colorado Desert now. Observe how much the vegetation (and temperature) has changed.

High desert or low desert, the Park has an abundance of things that slink, crawl, jump and fly. Keep your eyes peeled for the shifty sidewinder rattlesnake. Give these critters a wide berth and you'll both be happier campers! If you have arachnophobia you'll want to avoid a face-to-face meeting with our larger-than-life desert friend, aphonopelma chalcodes. That's the big furry guy with all those legs - the tarantula.

There's plenty of amusing animal life in the Park as well: the ever-present lizards, quail, road runners and coyotes. Speaking of coyotes, DON'T feed these "Help me, I look so pitiful" coyotes. You'll see them working the roads and campgrounds like some of those panhandlers you find on the street corners in metropolitan areas. We even spotted one who seemed to have an injured left back paw – except when he encountered a new set of tourists, he now seemed to have an injured *right* back paw.

The Park is the home of the seldom seen Desert Tortoise. The tortoises are a federally protected endangered specie. In the last 20 years, Desert Tortoise populations have declined by 90 percent. If you see one of these fellows lumbering along on the road, take care not to run it down. If you can, safely pull off the road and move the tortoise to a safer location.

The Joshua Tree Tortoise Rescue folks suggest that you "Walk over to the tortoise, letting it see you approaching. Lift it slowly and gently, keeping it level and low to the ground. Move it to a safe place off the road, no more than 100 yards away, in the same direction it was traveling. Carefully set it down, preferably in the shade of a shrub. It is imperative not to frighten the tortoise so that it does not void its vital internal water supply. DON'T take it home and DON'T feed it."

(Source: Joshua Tree Turtle & Tortoise Rescue)

Coyote

Tarantula

Cholla Cacti

If you see a sick or injured tortoise please report it to Tortoise Rescue at (760) 369-1235. They will come and pick up the injured tortoise. For more information on the Desert tortoise visit their website at:

http://www.desertusa.com/june96/tortoiserescue.html.

Least we forget, never leave food out at your campsite when you're gone. It invites unwanted visitors like ravens and coyotes, and helps create bad habits for the animals. One time we left our plastic gallon water jug sitting out on the picnic table and returned to find it nearly empty. After silently cursing nearby campers for being so low as to steal our water we discovered the real culprits – seems like "bee"ing so low was the key to our dilemma. The bees were repeatedly stinging the plastic jug and getting water! Anyway, if you're allergic to bee stings, beware (not a pun) when you're around the trash dumpsters as the bees like to hang around these and get whatever they get from soft drink cans. The Park has posted signs alerting campers to this potential danger.

Of course the Park has its share of eagles, hawks and owls. Watch as they cruise the skies looking for that next meal of rabbit, squirrel or other unlucky animal they happen to sight. The owls make delightful night sounds as they call out, "who's calling who". Speaking of the night, don't cheat yourself out of one of the Park's biggest spectacles - the night sky. We were at the Park when the Hale-Bobb comet was passing earth and it was a sight to behold. We never did figure out if those bright things trailing the comet were quarter dollar coins!

Well, this is a book about rock climbing so we're not going to try to give you a natural history lesson, but you can see there's a lot of interesting stuff in the Park to learn about. So, pick up some of the reading material about the desert at a Park visitor center or in town; there's more to this place than meets the eye.

Joshua tree along the Wonderland Trail

Desert Tortoise

Rock Art

Old Adobe

PARK HISTORY

Joshua Tree National Monument was created on August 10, 1936 by Presidential Proclamation of Franklin D. Roosevelt.

While its name remained unchanged over the years, its size did not. Various proclamations and acts of Congress added more area to the National Monument.

In March 1984, the Monument was included as part of a "Biosphere Reserve" system which included Death Valley National Monument and several other southwestern areas.

Never heard of a Biosphere Reserve? Well, we hadn't either. Someone suggested that it was a backup quarterback for the Miami Dolphins. We doubted that, so we dug into the mystery and surfaced with these facts.

"Biosphere reserves are set aside by the United Nations Education, Scientific, and Cultural Organization under its Man and the Biosphere Program (MAB). MAB was started with the intention to test and outline how humans can strike a balance among the apparently conflicting issues of conserving biological diversity, promoting economic and social development, and maintaining associated cultural values. A proposed reserve is nominated by its national government and must meet a minimum set of criteria. Individual biosphere reserves remain under the sovereign jurisdiction of the countries in which they are situated."

(source: Joshua Tree National Park Strategic Mission Statement)

So, now we know.

It wasn't until October 31, 1994 that Joshua Tree National Monument was elevated to National Park status. President Bill Clinton included it in the California Desert Protection Act as part of the largest protected wilderness area established in the lower 48 states.

Joshua trees

The promotion of Joshua Tree to be a National Park was a significant event for which we can all be ever thankful to President Clinton, but we shall always remember a couple of other events he initiated: the removal of the dreaded 55 mile per hour speed limit and allowing Global Positioning Satellite units to operate without those nasty selective availability errors.

(Sources: All Joshua Tree National Park information is courtesy of the government's Joshua Tree website at http://www.nps.gov/jotr/)

VISITOR INFORMATION

CONTACT INFORMATION:
Phone: (760) 367-5500   **Email:** JOTR_Info@nps.gov
Fax: (760) 367-6392   **Web:** http://www.nps.gov/jotr
Physical address: 74485 National Park Drive, Twentynine Palms, CA 92277-3597
Joshua Tree National Park is open to the public every day of the year.

LOCATION: Where in the world is Joshua Tree National Park? If you were (or are) a Marine you would know the Park is located near Twentynine Palms in southern California, just north of the Salton Sea.

HOW TO GET THERE: See map (page 8 & 9).

CLIMATE AND WEATHER: Flash floods, earthquakes, fires, wind, rain, snow, etc.. Don't climb if you can't take a joke. In any given year it is possible to have to deal with any or all of these tricks of Mother Nature.

If you're planning a climbing trip to the Park, it's a good idea to call ahead and find out what conditions you might expect for the date you are planning to arrive. There are a couple of websites which give you good up-to-date weather information as well as a webcam for your viewing pleasure. These URL's may change by the time you read this, but here goes anyway:

www2.nature.nps.gov/air/webcams/parks/jotrcam/jotrcam.htm.
www.srh.noaa.gov/data/forecasts/CAZO28.php?warncounty=CACO71&city =Joshu

Check the above URL's to see what the weather forecasters think will be happening as averages don't mean much these days.

The best temperature reference that we have found is the temperature monitoring equipment located at the Lost Horse Ranger Station at 4100 feet (1,250m). The temperature is sampled hourly.

www.cdec.water.ca.gov/cgi-progs/queryF?LTH

Generally speaking, you should find spring temperatures around 80F (27C) during the day and 50F (10C) during the night. Fall temperatures can be a little warmer during the day but about the same at night. Days are usually sunny to partly cloudy. We've sweated or frozen ourselves from one year to the next during the same time period, so who knows? What we do know is that the weather forecast doesn't change the weather. Be prepared. Count on wind in spring. We've had a little more rainy weather in the fall than in the spring. Bring a good book to read and you'll be OK.

The heat and the wind can combine to produce significant dehydration, so be sure to drink plenty of water before you start guzzling down those cervezas after climbing. You'll feel better in the morning and your tongue won't be as thick!

Springtime sky

BEST TIME TO CLIMB: When is the best time to climb at JTree? Hopefully, whenever you can get away for a few days, a weekend or a month! Spring and fall are the best times of the year due to pleasant temperatures. Spring is especially beautiful with the proliferation of blooming Joshua Trees and cactus. Summer can be a burner and the rock gets "greasy," so unless you like climbing at night we would suggest postponing your trip until cooler weather prevails.

Spring break tends to be a very busy time and campsites are at a premium. Winter days can be warm but the nights are long and cold unless you have an understanding tent partner, a camper or are staying at one of the fine motels in Twentynine Palms or Joshua Tree. Crack climbing with cold hands can be interesting. Is my hand really in that crack?

We prefer March and April followed closely by October and November. You'll find that the temperature ranges for both periods are about the same. The added advantage of climbing in the Fall is the relative lack of wind. Winds in the desert peak in the springtime.

EMERGENCIES: In an emergency place a collect call to San Bernardino Dispatch at **(909) 383-5651**. You can also place an emergency call to the Park Rangers using the emergency phone located by the restroom in the Intersection Rock parking lot.

PARK FACILITIES

ENTRANCE STATIONS: There are currently three main entrance stations into Joshua Tree National Park proper. We have purposely omitted reference to Indian Cove as we have not referenced any climbs in that area.

West Entrance Station. Located southeast from the intersection of California highway 62 and Park Boulevard in the town of Joshua Tree.

North Entrance Station. Located south from the intersection of California highway 62 and Utah Trail on the east side of the town of Twentynine Palms. This is the location of the primary visitor center, Oasis of Mara Visitor Center.

South Entrance Station. Located approximately 25 miles (40 km) east of Indio, CA and approximately 75 miles (120 km) west of Blythe, CA north from I-10.

ENTRANCE FEES: The Park follows the fee guidelines set forth by the National Park System. Specifically, the fees are as follows:

Vehicles	$10 for 7 consecutive days
Walk-Ins/Bikes	$5 for 7 consecutive days
Joshua Tree Pass	$25 for 12 months
National Parks Pass	$50 good for one full year from date of first use
Golden Age/Golden Access Pass	Free admittance (Free at last!)

The Park takes major credit cards.

VISITOR CENTERS: Park Visitor Centers: Both Park visitor centers are closed on Christmas Day.

The Oasis of Mara Visitor Center (open from 8:00 AM to 5:00 PM: extended hours during some periods). This location is the larger of the two Park Visitor Centers and features a host of exhibits as well as a nature walk. Water is available at this facility both free and for purchase for RV users. You'll also find public flush toilets, exhibits, a bookstore and a telephone (located east across the parking lot from the main building).

The Cottonwood Visitor Center (open from 8:00 AM to 5:00 PM). It is the smaller of the two visitor centers. There are public flush toilets, exhibits and a bookstore at this facility. There is NOT a public telephone at this location. Water is located in the Cottonwood Spring Campground south of the visitor center.

CAMPGROUNDS: *Always* check with the Park Rangers at the visitor centers or entrance stations regarding rules and regulations within the Park as they can change at any time.

The Park has 9 established campgrounds. There is a 30-day camping limit each year. During the period October through May there is a 14 consecutive day camping limitation.

There is a 2 vehicle, 3 tent, 6 person limit per non-group site. The Rangers will roust you out in the middle of the night to move that third vehicle. Been there, done that!

The table below summarizes the campgrounds/facilities within the Park.

Campground	# of Sites	Water?	Fee?	Reservations?
White Tank	15	No	$5 per night	No
Belle	18	No	$5 per night	No
Ryan	31	No	$5 per night	No
Hidden Valley	45	No	$5 per night	No
Cottonwood	62	Yes	$10 per night	No
Black Rock	100	Yes	$10 per night	(800) 365-2267
Indian Cove	101	No	$10 per night	(800) 365-2267
Jumbo Rocks	125	No	$5 per night	No
Sheep Pass	Group Camp	No	Yes - varies	(800) 365-2267

Campers at Hidden Valley, Ryan, Jumbo Rocks, Belle and White Tank campgrounds are required to fill out a "fee envelope". Enclose the appropriate campsite fee and place the envelope in an "iron ranger". Follow any further instructions on the fee envelope for showing that you've paid for your site. Golden Age and Golden Access pass holders receive a 50% discount on camping fees. No refunds will be made for overpayments or early departures.

Camp reservations can be made on the Web at **http://reservations.nps.go**v. Campgrounds and the Park are open all year.

GROUP CAMPGROUNDS: Group campgrounds are available on a reservation-only basis.

Sheep Pass is the main group campground within the Park. It has 6 group sites at $20-$35 per night. Cottonwood campground has 3 group sites at $25 per night. Indian Cove campground has 13 group sites at $20-$35 per night. Group sites may accommodate from 10 to 70 individuals.

IMPORTANT MISCELLANEOUS STUFF: Cottonwood and Indian Cove campgrounds are at the lowest elevation (warmer in winter/hotter in summer) while Hidden Valley, Ryan and Jumbo are among the highest. Indian Cove is a good place to climb when it is windy and cooler higher up.

Be advised that during the spring and fall, campsites begin to be fully occupied starting on Thursday evening and by Friday it's slim pickings. Forget trying to get a campsite on a Saturday evening. Your best bet is to find someone with only one vehicle at their campsite and ask if you can share their space. We have made some long lasting friendships that way. Those folks are probably sorry they ever said "Yes". Guess that gives more credence to "Just say No!".

Hidden Valley is the preferred camping area for climbers due to the multitude of routes within walking distance.

Emergency phone & restrooms

SERVICES WITHIN THE PARK

RESTROOMS: Restrooms are conveniently located throughout the Park. The Park has replaced all of the old pit toilets with nice, state-of-the-art, clean, sunny, virtually odorless, roomy chemical toilets (Yes!). You won't have to stand on the seats any more. Let's help keep them like new.

TELEPHONES: Within the Park, pay phones are located at the Oasis visitor center at Twentynine Palms and at Black Rock campground. There is NO public telephone at the Cottonwood Visitors Center.

An emergency-only phone is located by the restroom at the Intersection Rock parking lot located next to Hidden Valley Campground.

MESSAGE BOARDS: All campgrounds have message boards where you can leave messages on how your friends can find you or other trivia.

DRINKING WATER AND BEVERAGES: There is no drinking water source within the Park proper. You will find drinking water and some beverages located at the Visitor Centers. You will need to insure that you have an adequate supply of drinking water with you when you enter the Park. Water must be purchased at the west entrance station; there is no free supply. Free water is available at the Oasis of Mara Visitor Center and at the Cottonwood Spring Campground near the Cottonwood Spring Visitor Center. In all cases, you'll need to provide the water containers.

PICNIC AREAS: Picnic areas are conveniently located through the Park.

RECREATIONAL VEHICLES: RVs are welcome in all areas, but be aware that White Tank campground has a maximum vehicle length of 25 feet. Jumbo Rocks campground has a number of sites along its main road that can easily accommodate campers and RVs.

There are no RV hookups located within the Park. RV dump stations are available at Black Rock and Cottonwood campgrounds.

EMERGENCIES: In an emergency, place a collect call to San Bernardino Dispatch at **(909) 383-5651**.

The proliferation of cell phones should make it easier to locate a phone in the case of an emergency. However, familiarize yourself and your climbing partners with the location of the Intersection Rock parking lot emergency phone prior to climbing as minutes save lives in an emergency.

SERVICES OUTSIDE THE PARK

MOTELS: A number of small, independent motels operate in the towns of Twentynine Palms, Joshua Tree, and the larger Yucca Valley. In addition, the following nationally-known chains have motels in the area:

Holiday Inn Express, 71809 Twentynine Palms Highway, Twentynine Palms, CA 92277, (800) 465-4329

Best Western Garden Inn & Suites, 71487 Twentynine Palms Highway, Twentynine Palms, CA 92277, (760) 367-9141

Motel 6, 72562 Twentynine Palms Highway, Twentynine Palms, CA 92277, (760) 367-2833

RESTAURANTS: When you just can't deal with another night of eating Ramen noodles, try heading into town to one of our favorite spots, or explore and find other good things to eat.

On Twentynine Palms Highway, within the town of Twentynine Palms, try Edchada's (Mexican), Rocky's New York Style Pizza, or Rib Company (BBQ). In the town of Joshua Tree (also along the main highway), we like Royal Siam Cuisine (Thai) and Country Kitchen (for a really hearty breakfast). I'm getting hungry already!

Of course, you can also find familiar national chains such as Del Taco (we're regulars there), McDonald's, Burger King, Denny's, Jack in the Box, Pizza Hut, Subway, and Taco Bell, all in Twentynine Palms. Yucca Valley has an even greater selection of local and national restaurants, but is a bit further to drive.

GROCERIES: Is it time to stock up on Little Debbie's and beer? These and much more can be purchased at local grocery stores. Don't forget the ice!

Twentynine Palms: Stater Brother's Market is west of "downtown" Twentynine Palms on the main highway, south side of the road. Huge selection.

Desert Ranch Market is located in the midst of "downtown" Twentynine Palms, on the north side of the main highway across from Edchada's restaurant.

Joshua Tree: Sam's Market II is on the main highway, north side of the road. This is a small market, with limited selections. They might have your Little Debbie's and beer, however.

Joshua tree detail

Yucca Valley: Stater Brother's Market has a location near the east end of Yucca Valley (not far from Joshua Tree) on the Twentynine Palms Highway, north side of the road. Huge selection.

Von's is also located on the east side of Yucca Valley, also on the north side of the Twentynine Palms Highway. Another huge supermarket.

SHOWERS: Now that you've worked yourself into a frenzy climbing all of these really cool routes, you're going to need a shower to get rid of the dust and dirt. Convenient places which we have found are:

Joshua Tree: Coyote Corner at the intersection of Park Boulevard and Twentynine Palms Highway (very convenient to the West entrance to the park) is a unique little gift shop with clean, convenient showers for rent in an addition behind the main building. Obtain a key to one of the shower rooms from the clerk in the store. The showers are coin-operated (quarters), so you can keep plugging in money if you like a long shower. (760) 366-9683

Twentynine Palms: 29 Palms RV & Golf Resort is located on Amboy Road between Adobe Rd & Utah Trail. Access to the dressing rooms / showers is available 9 AM to dusk, and you can rent a shower for $5. There are several showers with small dressing areas in both the men's and women's dressing room.

Jerry's Gym also lets you rent a shower in their dressing rooms for $5 per person. There is only 1 shower per dressing room, so this might be a slow choice for a large group of climbers. To find Jerry's, head north from Twentynine Palms Highway on Adobe Road (Denny's is on the corner). Drive 1 mile to Two Mile Road, and turn right (east). The gym is about a block down the road on the left. (760) 361-8010

LAUNDROMAT: Twentynine Palms: Try the Alamo Laundromat on Adobe. A clean place with plenty of washers and dryers.

Joshua Tree: There's a laundromat located on the highway near Park Boulevard.

CLIMBING EQUIPMENT: Need some gear? Left your climbing shoes sitting on top of the car when you drove away from the house? Try:

Coyote Corner

Nomad Ventures. Intersection of Twentynine Palms Highway and Park Blvd (across the street from Coyote Corner) in the town of Joshua Tree. (760) 366-4684

They rent and sell almost anything you might need, and some things you don't need, but just have to buy because it looks "cool".

Also, Coyote Corner; they're across the street from Nomad Ventures (they also have showers for rent).

INTERNET ACCESS: For that ever-important email check, plus a Tall Espresso Macchiato with a shot of Hazelnut, stop in at Beatnik Coffee House. You can rent time on their computers while sipping some wonderful concoction. The Coffee House is located in the town of Joshua Tree on the main highway, next door to Royal Siam Cuisine.

EMERGENCIES: Outside of the Park, call 911 in an emergency.

GENERAL INFORMATION

DIRECTIONS: For the geographically challenged we've tried to designate directions using left and right instead of north-northeast or southwest, etc. To make things even easier to follow, you will find that we have not resorted to "walk 19 steps backwards" in the descriptions. Diane made me promise not to include the word "leap" in connection with scrambling over boulders.

EQUIPMENT: All climbs in this book require just a "standard rack" unless otherwise designated. A "standard rack" includes wired nuts and/or cams from small (but not "tiny") to 2.5". Include an assortment of quickdraws and slings for all climbs.

All of the routes can be climbed with either a single 50m or 60m rope. Unless we say otherwise, either length rope will work. Some routes may require that two ropes be used for the rappel.

ANCHORS: We suggest that you always use belay anchors at the top and bottom of climbs. Failure to do so can result in serious injury or death to the belayer and/or the lead climber. More than one belayer has become "one with the rock" when the lead climber falls and the belayer did not have a secure anchor.

We frequently make reference to "Create your own" in relation to upper anchors. This statement always applies to the lower anchor. You will normally need to bring along a selection of long/medium slings to sling boulders at the bottom and top of the routes. Your anchor may also require a couple of nuts or camming devices. If possible, back up all fixed anchors due to possible unseen damage to the anchor.

Belayers: Don't forget those helmets. A dropped #2 camming device can put a nasty hole in the top of your skull and leave you unable to belay your leader.

We know that you are aware of this stuff but we all get a little careless now and then. Safety pays big dividends.

CLASS DEFINITIONS: (For Approaches and Descents)

Class 1: A "walk in the park" with your hands in your pockets.

Class 2: Some scrambling, using hands mainly for balance.

Class 3: Hand and feet used for climbing. A fall will usually result in a serious case of "rock rash" and possible broken bones. You may want the use of a rope.

Class 4: You are definitely climbing. A fall will usually result in serious injury or death. Using a rope is a smart idea.

Class 5: Hopefully you've noticed that the approach is complete and it's time to rack up and climb the route!

DESCENTS: Okay, you've just finished the climb. Now what? How do you get back down to the start of the route? We once got stuck on top of a climb for quite some time because we didn't do our homework about getting off the climb. So, we have included the descent information for every climb in the Guide.

Most of the descents in this Guide involve some class 3 down climbing which can result in serious injury, or worse, if you fall. Don't down climb anything unroped if you don't feel confident in your ability to do so. We suggest belaying all 4th class down climbs. Only you know your down climbing ability.

JUST FOR FUN: Climbing is fun and we would like to help you keep it that way, which is why we wrote this guide book. In that vein, we have compiled a list of routes on a geographical basis with minimal approach times and a maximum amount of climbing time. The notable exception is Mental Physics, which has about a 1 hour approach into Wonderland of Rocks. However, it is such a fine climb that we couldn't imagine leaving it out.

Rappelling

Top belay

SAFETY

SAFETY ISSUES: Neither this nor any other guidebook can protect you from injury or death. You must take responsibility for your own actions. Always be willing and ready to back off a route if it looks too difficult or if the weather is threatening.

You should be competent leading traditional climbs of the difficulty described in this Guide. If not, obtain professional guided instruction or climb with a leader you know who has demonstrated their ability to lead the climbs described in this Guide.

Information regarding professional climbing guiding/instruction can be obtained at one of the following:

Joshua Tree Rock Climbing School
HCR Box 3034, Joshua Tree CA 92252
(760) 366-4745 or (800) 890-4745
Email: climb@telis.org

Vertical Adventures®, Inc.
(800) 514-8785 or (949) 854-6250
Email: Bgvertical@aol.com

Nomad Ventures
Located at the corner of Highway 62
and Park Blvd., Joshua Tree, CA
(760) 366-4684

Coyote Corner
Located at the corner of Highway 62
and Park Blvd., Joshua Tree, CA
(760) 366-9683

We're not going to attempt to tell you how to climb, but we do want to stress a few fundamental safety issues.

READY TO START THE ROUTE: Helmets on? Ready to go? We always have our partner check our harness and knots prior to starting the climb. It just takes a minute and may save a lifetime. Do the same for your partner.

Placing bi-directional (opposing) pieces of protection at the bottom of your route will help prevent the pieces from "zippering" out in the event of a fall. We know of more than one case where protection has zippered.

READY FOR THE RAPPEL/DOWNCLIMB: Things change. Someone may install a new anchor at the top of a formation, or an anchor may become unsafe and disappear over time due to weather or human actions. Always inspect an existing anchor before trusting it, and be prepared to find an alternate descent if an anchor doesn't look safe.

The first climber to reach the ground should always ensure that the rope can be easily retrieved while their partner is still at the top of the route. You'll be a happier camper if you do this. We've had to climb back up the route/rope on several occasions and it isn't always that much fun - trust us.

We don't claim to have discovered the "best" downclimb from every route. Your level of experience and comfort with exposure may lead you to find a different way down than what we describe.

SLEEPING BAG: Don't forget to check that sleeping bag for tarantulas before turning in. It could be a life altering experience to feel one climbing up your leg after you've zipped up for the night!

GETTING LOST: It is easy to get disoriented (a.k.a. "lost") while hiking to your climb, particularly in the Wonderland of Rocks area. After a while all of those rocks can look alike. We commonly refer to this as the "Wanderland" of Rocks. In 2003 a hiker became lost on a nature trail loop near Barker Dam and was not found for several days. He narrowly escaped dying. He had slipped down between some rocks while looking around to see where he was. He did not have food or water and suffered some injuries that prevented him from climbing back up the rock to safety. Don't let this happen to you!

Climb safely and enjoy many sun and fun filled days of climbing at Joshua Tree.

ENVIRONMENTAL & ETHICAL RESPONSIBILITIES

Preserve and protect our natural resources. Familiarize yourself with the concerns addressed in the Joshua Tree National Park Backcountry and Wilderness Management Plan. Give special attention to the section entitled Climbing Management. The full text can be found on the web at http://www.nps.gov/jotr/manage/bcmp/plnframe.html.

This document deals with the impact that climbers have on the natural and cultural resources as well as the experiences of other visitors as a result of climbers' actions.

Specifically, chipping or altering the rock in any manner is expressly forbidden - and with good reason. Bolting (which trad climbers don't use) is strictly controlled.

Take care to use established trails. The Access Fund and California Native Plant Society have been very proactive in establishing climbers' trails - use them.

Damage to plant life at the base of the climbs is another issue of concern to Park management. It should also be our concern as climbers.

Jay

Due to its visibility, the use of chalk is an ongoing environmental problem. Chalk use can quickly become unsightly and an area of concern to other visitors. Most visitors (and climbers) can't always spot those bolts but chalk streaks on the rock are very visible. Limit your use of chalk.

It is prohibited to climb within 50 feet of any rock-art site.

It is prohibited to initiate or terminate a climb in an occupied campsite without prior permission of the occupant of that site.

These are but a few of the issues covered in the Management Plan, Alternative "E". Climb responsibly and be a responsible climber. Do your part and go a step further by helping to educate your climbing partners in responsible climbing techniques.

While it's not specifically mentioned in the Management Plan, leaving your blood and bone fragments at the bottom of the climb is considered defacing the rock and littering; we strongly discourage this.

Diane climbing

Echo Rock at sunset

EQUIPMENT

So you're finally going to make that weeklong climbing trip out to JTree. Well now, here are a few things you might want to throw into the back of the vehicle to make camp life more enjoyable:

CLOTHING:

- T-Shirt
- Shorts
- Long sleeve shirt (for those cooler days)
- Long climbing pants
- Ball cap/climbing cap
- Jacket (for cool evenings)
- Wind shell (for cool windy afternoons)
- Light weight gloves (for cool evenings)
- Extra underwear

Junior rangers examine the rack

SLEEPING:

- Tent & fly (if tent camping - hey, it may rain!)
- Tent poles & stakes
- Ground cloth
- Sleeping pad
- Sleeping bag
- Headlamp / extra batteries
- Ear plugs (softens wind and Hidden Valley CG noise)
- Pillow (unless you have an understanding climbing partner)

COOKING AND EATING:

- Water (multiple 1-2.5 gallon containers - fill at entrance station)
- Stove/Fuel (propane is convenient)
- Pots/pans
- Cooking/eating utensils
- Paper plates
- Paper towels
- Knife/cutting board
- Colander (handy for pasta and those delicious salads)
- Bottle opener (those beer bottle caps are hard on the teeth!)
- Corkscrew
- Plastic trash bags
- Stuff to clean up those pots & pans
- Cooler

FOOD:

- Local supermarkets are convenient
- Snacks (for climbing)
- Cookies (remember, you're on vacation)
- Chocolate (the foundation of the food pyramid)
- Gatorade/Sports drinks (keep hydrated)
- Beer/Spirits (to counteract the effects of the Gatorade)

CLIMBING:

- Helmet (don't be macho - helmets save lives)
- Rope(s) - 50/60m
- Rope bag (that sand will eat up your rope)
- Climbing harness
- Belay/Rappel device
- Rock shoes (pain is your friend)
- Climbing rack (your choice here - mark your stuff)
- Slings/Webbing
- Chalk or Bison Ball
- Sports Tape (those cracks hurt like hell!)
- Small backpack
- Water bottle(s)
- Courage (bring some extra for your partner)
- Guidebook(s)

KEEPING CLEAN AND HEALTHY:

- Wash cloth (dipped in heated water, placed on the face in the AM is great!)
- Bath towel (you are going to bathe aren't you?)
- Solar shower (feels great after a hard day of climbing)
- Toothbrush, toothpaste, floss (be considerate of your climbing partners)
- "No Rinse" shampoo (try it, you'll like it)
- Liquid Hand Sanitizer (Kill them germs)
- Personal hygiene articles
- Toilet paper (just in case someone stole 10 rolls from the closest restroom)
- First Aid kit
- Pain killer (ibuprofen - "Vitamin i"- aspirin, Yukon Jack, etc.)

MISCELLANEOUS:

- Climbing partner(s)
- Sun glasses
- Sunscreen (SPF 30)
- Lip sunscreen (SPF 15)
- Band-Aid® Liquid Bandage (good for those nasty "finger cracks")
- Foot deodorant (those rock shoes get really stinky)
- Gym bag for dirty clothes after showering
- Reading material (Leave the Wall Street Journal at home)
- Duct tape (the universal fixer-upper)
- Camera & film or Digital camera (extra memory cards)
- Camp Lantern
- Windproof matches/lighter
- Wood for fire / fire starter / newspaper (OK, so you should have brought the Wall Street Journal!)
- Camp chairs (for sitting around the fire)
- Mountain bike (cross-training is fun)

Have we left anything out? You probably don't have any room left in your vehicle anyway. Send us your list and we'll make this one better.

Preparing to climb

Morning wash

JOSHUA TREE

SUN/SHADE SYMBOLS

"It's too hot to climb!"..... *Come on, let's just find some routes in the shade.*
"It's too cold; I can't feel my hands!"..... *All we need are some routes in the sun.*
"It's so windy, I can't stand up!"..... *OK, I give up. Let's go to town, hit the showers and chow down on some real food!*

Sound familiar? The only problem now is finding those shady or sunny climbs. We're here to help. We've taken compass readings on all the climbs in this book, and have compiled our findings in a chart. We've even come up with some handy graphics to help you quickly choose a sunny or shady climb. A sun means sunny; a black box means shady. A split box showing half a sun and half a black box means starting out sunny and becoming shady, or vice versa. In our chart, a Southwestern facing climb (SW) starts out shady in the early morning but turns sunny by late morning (AM). Then it stays sunny all afternoon (PM)

Here are the 8 possible combinations you'll see in this guide:

Afternoon shadows

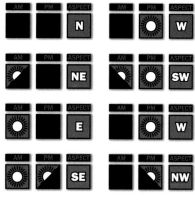

So far so good, except that the sun varies its path through the sky at different times of year. These general guidelines should be pretty accurate from late autumn through the winter and into early spring. During the hot months, even a North-facing climb may see sun early in the morning and late in the afternoon. Or a nearby crag may cast its shadow on your "sunny" climb for a few hours. Oh well just save that climb for another day.

Sun and shade
on Saddle Rock

CLIMBS BY SUN/SHADE

JOSHUA TREE

CLIMBS BY DIFFICULTY

ACCESS: IT'S EVERYONE'S CONCERN

The Access Fund is a national nonprofit climbers' organization working to keep climbing areas open and conserve the climbing environment. Need help with a climbing related issue? Call us and please consider these principles when climbing.

ASPIRE TO CLIMB WITHOUT LEAVING A TRACE: Especially in environmentally sensitive areas like caves. Chalk can be a significant impact. Pick up litter and leave trees and plants intact.

MAINTAIN A LOW PROFILE: Minimize noise and yelling at the crag.

DISPOSE OF HUMAN WASTE PROPERLY: Use toilets whenever possible. If toilets are not available, dig a "cat hole" at least six inches deep and 200 feet from any water, trails, campsites or the base of climbs. Always pack out toilet paper. Use a "poop tube" on big wall routes.

USE EXISTING TRAILS: Cutting switchbacks causes erosion. When walking off-trail, tread lightly, especially in the desert on cryptogamic soils.

BE DISCRETE WITH FIXED ANCHORS: Bolts are controversial and are not a convenience. Avoid placing unless they are absolutely necessary. Camouflage all anchors and remove unsightly slings from rappel stations.

RESPECT THE RULES: Speak up when other climbers do not. Expect restrictions in designated wilderness areas, rock art sites and caves. Power drills are illegal in wilderness and all national parks.

PARK AND CAMP IN DESIGNATED AREAS: Some climbing areas require a permit for overnight camping.

RESPECT PRIVATE PROPERTY: Be courteous to landowners.

JOIN THE ACCESS FUND: To become a member, make a tax-deductible donation of $35.

ACCESS FUND
your climbing future
www.accessfund.org

P.O. Box 17010
Boulder, CO 80308
303 545 6772

Evening light

LOST HORSE AREA

1 Just Another Roadside Attraction
2 Granny Goose
3 Maggie's Farm
4 Rainy Day Women
5 Cake Walk
6 Dinkey Doinks
7 Young Lust
8 Smithereens
9 Double Dogleg
10 Beck's Bet
11 Mr. Michael Goes To Washington
12 The Swift
13 Dappled Mare
14 Solar Technology
15 Men with Cow's Heads
16 Classic Corner
17 Dr. Seuss Vogel
18 Roboranger
19 Beck's Bear
20 Practice Rehearsal
21 Scrumdillyishus
22 Frosty Cone
23 Mr. Misty Kiss
24 Overseer
25 Dung Fu
26 White Lightning
27 Feltoneon Physics

● 5.5 / 5.6   ■ 5.7   ■ 5.8   ◆ 5.9

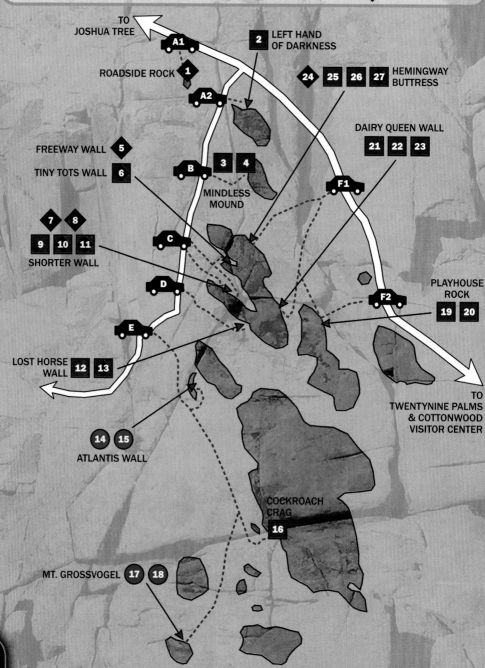

TO JOSHUA TREE

A1

ROADSIDE ROCK   1

A2

2 LEFT HAND OF DARKNESS

24 25 26 27 HEMINGWAY BUTTRESS

DAIRY QUEEN WALL
21 22 23

FREEWAY WALL   5
TINY TOTS WALL   6

B   3 4

MINDLESS MOUND

F1

7 8
9 10 11
SHORTER WALL

C

D

E

LOST HORSE WALL   12 13

F2

PLAYHOUSE ROCK
19 20

TO TWENTYNINE PALMS & COTTONWOOD VISITOR CENTER

14 15
ATLANTIS WALL

COCKROACH CRAG
16

MT. GROSSVOGEL   17 18

LOST HORSE AREA - ACCESS

PARKING: **A1** **A2**

FORMATIONS: Roadside Rock (for Route **1** Just another Roadside Attraction)
Left Hand of Darkness (for Route **2** Granny Goose)

LOCATION: These two formations are located only 0.1 mile (0.2 km) apart, and there are parking spots next to each. To park closest to **Left Hand of Darkness**, pull into the parking area **(A2)** located on Lost Horse Road at the intersection with Park Boulevard. Left Hand of Darkness is the formation directly in front of your parked car.

To park closer to **Roadside Rock**, start at the intersection of Park Boulevard and Lost Horse Road, and drive 0.1 miles (0.2 km) north along Park Boulevard (toward the town of Joshua Tree) to the first parking pullout **(A1)** on the left side of the road.

As the name of the rock indicates, this small formation is very close to the road (on the "Roadside")

Roadside Rock as seen from the parking pullout A 1 on Park Boulevard

TO ROADSIDE ROCK:
Approach: Class 1
From the pullout next to Roadside Rock, walk back along Park Boulevard a very short distance to the start of the route, which faces the road.

TO LEFT HAND OF DARKNESS:
Approach: Class 1
From the parking area by the intersection follow a short path marked with an Access Fund sign to the start of the route.

Left Hand of Darkness as seen from the parking area A2 on Lost Horse Road next to the intersection with Park Boulevard.

PARKING: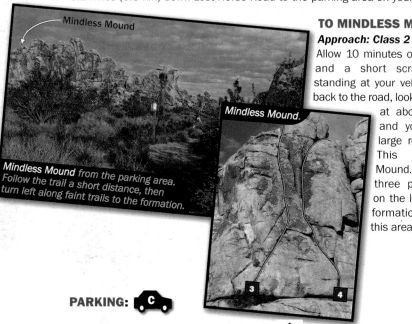

FORMATIONS: Mindless Mound (for Route **3** Maggie's Farm, and Route **4** Rainy Day Women)

LOCATION: From the intersection of Park Boulevard and Lost Horse Road, drive 0.2 miles (0.3 km) down Lost Horse Road to the parking area on your left.

Mindless Mound

Mindless Mound *from the parking area. Follow the trail a short distance, then turn left along faint trails to the formation.*

Mindless Mound.

TO MINDLESS MOUND:
Approach: Class 2
Allow 10 minutes of easy walking and a short scramble. While standing at your vehicle with your back to the road, look off to your left at about 10 o'clock and you will see a large rock formation. This is Mindless Mound. You will notice three parallel cracks on the left end of this formation. Head for this area.

PARKING:

FORMATIONS: Freeway Wall (for Route **5** Cake Walk)
Tiny Tots Rock (for Route **6** Dinkey Doinks)
Shorter Wall (for Route **7** Young Lust, Route **8** Smithereens,
Route **9** Double Dogleg, Route **10** Beck's Bet,
and Route **11** Mr. Michael Goes to Washington)

LOCATION: From the intersection of Park Boulevard and Lost Horse Road, drive 0.3 mile (0.5 km) down Lost Horse Road to the parking area on your left. From this parking spot, you can make your way to Freeway Wall, Tiny Rock and/or Shorter Wall.

TO FREEWAY WALL AND TINY TOTS ROCK:
Approach: Class 2
Allow 15 minutes for a scramble up a boulder field. Leave the parking area and follow the trail for 200 yards or so until you encounter a small man-made dam. Turn left at this point to begin working your way up through the boulders to the tree located at the base of the Freeway Wall. Stay near the base of the wall as you hike up to the start of Cake Walk, the prominent dog leg crack about half-way along the upper wall. The feature up high on the horizon to the right of the climb resembles a diving board when seen from the road.

Dinkey Doinks is an easy scramble from the start of Cake Walk across boulders to the formation on your right, Tiny Tots Rock. The route is located near the right center of the face.

TO "UPPER" SHORTER WALL

Approach: Class 2

Allow 30 minutes for a scramble through the boulders. Leave the parking area and follow the trail until you encounter a small man-made dam. Stop here and study the terrain above. In the middle of the boulder field in front of you there is a tall, mostly dead, tree. In line with the tree and on the skyline you will see a prominent rock.

Work your way up through the jumble of boulders heading in a direction just left of the large tree and in line with the prominent rock. Resist the temptation to traverse over to the right wall prior to getting up even with the start of your climb as the scrambling gets much more difficult. There is no really simple way to get there; just keep scrambling up until you have located the upper wall.

TO "LOWER" SHORTER WALL

Approach: Class 2

Allow 10 minutes for an easy scramble through the boulders. Leave the parking area and walk down the road to where a well-defined trail heads away from the road about 30 yards to the right. Follow the trail toward the lower formation on your right. Scramble parallel to the base of this formation, keeping low in the minor gully until you are underneath a spot where a large boulder sits on top of the wall. This spot is parallel to the large, semi-dead tree off to your left. Head right, and make your way over the formation.

"Upper" Shorter Wall.

"Lower" Shorter Wall.

Freeway Wall   Tint Tots Rock

"Upper" Shorter Wall

"Lower" Shorter Wall

If you enjoy boulder hopping, you'll love the approaches to **Freeway Wall, Tiny Tots Rock,** and **Shorter Wall,** all in an area sometimes called the Rock Garden Valley.

PARKING: 🚗 **D**

FORMATIONS: Lost Horse Wall (for Route **12** The Swift, and Route **13** Dappled Mare)

LOCATION: From the intersection of Park Boulevard and Lost Horse Road, drive 0.5 miles (0.8km) down Lost Horse Road to the parking area on your left.

TO LOST HORSE WALL:

Approach: Class 2

Allow 10 minutes for the approach. Follow the trail for 50 yards as it leaves the parking area and drops down into the wash. Follow the wash up to the point where you see a large black circle about halfway up the left hand wall. Leave the wash here and scramble up through the rocks to the start of the climbs.

Roan Way

Lost Horse Wall

12

13

Lost Horse Wall

Lost Horse Wall is the massive formation on the left side of this 'valley'. The climbs are all toward the right end of the wall as you face it from the wash.

PARKING: 🚗 **E**

FORMATIONS: Atlantis Wall (for Route **14** Solar Technology, and Route **15** Men with Cow's Heads)
Cockroach Crag (for Route **16** Classic Corner/False Classic Corner)
Mt. Grossvogel (for Route **17** Dr. Seuss Vogel, and Route **18** Roboranger)

LOCATION: From the intersection of Park Boulevard and Lost Horse Road, drive 0.6 miles (1km) along Lost Horse Road to the parking area on your right. This is the last parking lot on Lost Horse Road that is available for visitor parking. The road beyond this point is closed to all non-official traffic.

Follow the trail as it leaves the parking area on the opposite side of the road. Keep to the left of the drainage. There are many trails in this area but generally parallel the formations on your left.

Begin your hike to **Atlantic Wall, Cockroach Crag,** and **Mt. Grossvogel** on a trail that starts left of the "Service Road" sign, and stays left of a large wash.

Down climb back to trail — Atlantis Wall

You can scope out your down climb - the area between the 2 parallel walls above - as you circle around to the right to reach the face of the **Atlantis Wall.**

TO ATLANTIS WALL:
Approach: Class 1
Allow 10 minutes walking on trail. Hike parallel to the formation on your left until you reach an obvious split in the trail. Bear left at this point to circle around the formation, passing a series of parallel walls. Once past these walls, turn left into a valley defined by a steep wall on the left side and a huge jumble of boulders in front of a formation on the right side. Follow the well-defined trail up and over some boulders to a point about two-thirds of the way along the wall.

TO COCKROACH CRAG:
Approach: Class 2
Allow 25 minutes walking on trails and a scramble up boulders. Follow the trail as it leaves the parking area on the opposite side of the road. Keep to the left of the drainage. There are many trails in this area, but generally parallel the formations on your left.

Follow the trail from the parking lot past the split in the trail for Atlantis Wall. Stay to the right at the split, and continue to follow a trail that parallels the series of large formations on your left. About the time you think you're lost, you should see a striking formation called the "Aiguille de Joshua Tree" just ahead **(Please see photo on page 73).**

Approximately 100 yards beyond the Aiguille make an abrupt turn to the left to head up to Classic Corner and False Classic Corner. Scramble up boulders behind the medium sized tree. Generally follow a line which heads up toward the two Yuccas, bear left and scramble up to the base of the climbs.

Atlantis Wall.

False Classic Corner — Classic Corner

False Classic Corner can be spotted above you near the skyline on **Cockroach Crag**, with **Classic Corner** just out of sight to its right.

Mt. Grossvogel comes into view shortly after you pass Aiguille de Joshua Tree.

Mt. Grossvogel

Descent

18

17

Mt. Grossvogel offers some shady and usually uncrowded options.

TO MT. GROSSVOGEL:

Approach: Class 1

Allow 25 minutes walking on trails. Follow the trail from the parking area past the split in the trail for Atlantis Wall. Stay right at the split continuing to follow a trail that parallels the series of formations on your left. About the time you're beginning to wonder if you've walked too far, you should see a needle-like formation called the "Aiguille de Joshua Tree" (5.6X) just ahead. How appropriate: aiguille translates as "needle"!

Approximately 40 yards beyond the Aiguille, begin looking to your right and you'll start to see a formation come into view in the distance. Make a sharp turn to the right. Head toward the formation in the distance. You will pass between two formations and cross a wash as you proceed to the climbs.

PARKING: [F1] [F2]

FORMATIONS: Playhouse Rock (for Route **19** Beck's Bear, and Route **20** Practice Rehearsal)
Dairy Queen Wall (for Route **21** Scrumdillyishus, Route **22** Frosty Cone, and Route **23** Mr. Misty Kiss)
Hemingway Buttress (for Route **24** Overseer, Route **25** Dung Fu, Route **26** White Lightning, and Route **27** Feltoneon Physics.

LOCATION: From the intersection of Hidden Valley Road and Park Boulevard, drive 0.9 miles (1.4 km) on Park Boulevard toward Lost Horse Road to the signed "Hemingway" parking lot **(F1)**. Allow 10 - 15 minutes of easy walking across the desert on easy-to-follow Access Fund trails. A trail leads to the base of Playhouse Rock, Dairy Queen Wall and Hemingway Buttress. Both require a scramble up some boulders.

To Playhouse Rock

Dairy Queen Wall

Hemingway Buttress

Playhouse Rock, Dairy Queen Wall, and Hemingway Buttress are accessible from the Hemingway parking lot.

TO PLAYHOUSE ROCK:

Approach: Class 1

Allow 5 minutes for the approach. Park in the Hemingway parking lot, or, if this is the only formation you plan to climb on today, park in the next pullout along Park Boulevard beyond the Hemingway lot as you head toward Intersection Rock (F2).

Follow the trail to the formation. Head over to the tallest tree located next to the wall.

TO DAIRY QUEEN WALL:

Approach: Class 2

Allow 15 minutes of easy walking on a good trail followed by a scramble up some boulders. Follow the marked climber's trail as it leaves the Hemingway parking lot just to the right of the restroom. Soon you will come to a marked fork in the trail. Take the left fork and hike toward the base of the boulders below the wall. Take the line of least resistance, starting to the left of the routes, then working your way up to the base of the climbs. You'll be a happier camper if you wear approach shoes with sticky soles for the last part of the approach.

TO HEMINGWAY BUTTRESS:

Approach: Class 2

Allow 15 minutes of easy walking on a good trail followed by a scramble up some boulders. Follow the marked climber's trail as it leaves the Hemingway parking lot just to the right of the restroom. Soon you will come to a marked fork in the trail. Take the right fork and hike over toward the base of the boulders below the wall. Follow the line of least resistance and scramble your way up to the bottom of the routes.

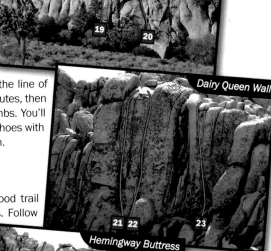

Playhouse Rock

19   20

Dairy Queen Wall

21 22   23

Hemingway Buttress

24   25   26   27

ROUTE 1

JUST ANOTHER ROADSIDE ATTRACTION

DIFFICULTY: 5.9 / 1 pitch

LOCATION: A1

Lost Horse Area
Roadside Rock Parking

SUN / SHADE:

AM	PM	ASPECT
◐	■	NE

APPROACH: *Class 1*
From the pullout on Park Boulevard, walk back along Park Boulevard a very short distance to the start of the route, which faces the road.

EQUIPMENT: Pro to 3".

UPPER BELAY: Create your own.

DESCENT: *Class 3*
Down climb back away from the route and slightly to your left. Follow a prominent gully as it descends back down toward the road.

GENERAL INFORMATION: This is one of those short climbs you can do at the end of the day. It doesn't look like a 5.9 (and maybe it isn't) but it does have a nasty little surprise for you up toward the top of the route - a little overhanging section which will make you wish you left with the rest of the gang to tip a few cool ones!

Joshua trees & yuccas

ROUTE DESCRIPTION: Scramble up to the bottom of the main crack. From here the route follows the crack up past the overhanging section to an enjoyable finish. This route is slightly overhanging near the top. There are abundant opportunities for placing protection on this route.

ROUTE NOTES:

Date Climbed: Led By:

Climbing Partners:

LOST HORSE AREA

ROUTE 2

GRANNY GOOSE

DIFFICULTY: 5.7 / 1 pitch

SUN / SHADE:

AM PM ASPECT

LOCATION:

Lost Horse Area
Left Hand of Darkness Parking

APPROACH: *Class 1*

This formation is located at the southeast corner of Park Boulevard and Lost Horse Road. The route is on the right end of the formation as you stand with your back toward Park Boulevard.

EQUIPMENT: Medium/large set of stoppers and/or camming devices.

UPPER BELAY: Pro to 3.5".

DESCENT: *Class 3*

Scramble up and back away from the climb, then work your way around to the left side of the formation and back toward the low point. Down climb off to the left and scramble through boulders back to the start of the climb.

GENERAL INFORMATION: The traverse and wide vertical crack offer an interesting variety to this route. It can be quite popular due to the ease of access.

Other routes in the area: Just Another Roadside Attraction (5.9), Maggie's Farm (5.7) and Rainy Day Women (5.7).

ROUTE DESCRIPTION: Climb up a broken section on the right end of the face to the start of the traverse. Plug in some pro under the flake as you move left across to the start of a wide vertical crack. Watch for features inside the crack and along its edges to help make your way up.

Try not to get your knee stuck on small features hidden within the crack! Some climbers prefer to exit the crack to the right as they leave the top of the crack to take advantage of some large features on the rock just before the finish of the climb.

Climbing Granny Goose

ROUTE NOTES:

Date Climbed: Led By:

Climbing Partners:

ROUTE 3

MAGGIE'S FARM

DIFFICULTY: 5.7 / 1 pitch

LOCATION:

Lost Horse Area
Mindless Mound Parking

SUN / SHADE:

APPROACH: *Class 2*

Study the rock face as you approach it. You will notice three parallel cracks on the left end of this formation. The third crack to the left is Maggie's Farm.

Scramble up among the boulders to the start of the route that is at the left end of a ledge by a bush.

EQUIPMENT: Standard Rack.

UPPER BELAY: Create your own.

DESCENT: *Class 2*

Down climb into the notch on your right as you face the route. When you get through the notch turn left and down climb the gully, finishing off and around to your left to reach the ground near the start of the route.

GENERAL INFORMATION: Both this route and Rainy Day Women get their names from Bob Dylan songs.

This route is a little off of the beaten path but is a fun climb. This climb and its neighbor, Rainy Day Women, are fun warm-up climbs. They are convenient if you have a group of four climbers as you can swap routes with your friends. You won't see other climbers here very often, so it can be a good alternative climb for those busy weekend days.

ROUTE DESCRIPTION: This route can optionally be started below and to the left of the crack. Climb up and right to the bottom of the crack through some easy moves. Good hand jams take you up toward the top of the climb to a slightly more difficult flaring crack section. Once past here, make a few easier moves to the top of the climb for fun climbing and good protection.

ROUTE NOTES:

Date Climbed: Led By:

Climbing Partners:

ROUTE 4

RAINY DAY WOMEN

DIFFICULTY: 5.7 / 1 pitch

LOCATION:

Lost Horse Area
Mindless Mound Parking

SUN / SHADE:

APPROACH: *Class 2*
You will notice three parallel cracks on the left end of Mindless Mound. Your route is the rightmost crack and is readily identifiable by the brownish color of the rock toward the top of the climb.

Scramble up among the boulders to the start of the route that is at the right end of a ledge.

EQUIPMENT: Pro to 3".

UPPER BELAY: Create your own.

DESCENT: *Class 2*
Down climb into the notch on your right as you face the route. When you get through the notch, turn left and down climb the gully, finishing off and around to your left to reach the ground near the start of the route.

GENERAL INFORMATION: If the name of this route sounds familiar, it should be. As Bob Dylan declared, "I would not feel so all alone, Everybody must get stoned." Let's go check out this stone.

This route is a little off the beaten path but is a fun climb. This climb and its neighbor, Maggie's Farm, are fun warm up climbs. Two climbing teams can egg each other on as they climb side by side. These are often good choices when the crowds get too big in other areas of the Park.

Joshua Trees

ROUTE DESCRIPTION: Climb up through an awkward off-width section to get up to the main crack. Some fine hand jams take you up toward the top of the route for one not-so-difficult crux move on the climb. Fun climbing and plenty of opportunities for placing protection.

ROUTE NOTES:

Date Climbed: Led By:

Climbing Partners:

ROUTE ◆5

DIFFICULTY: 5.9 / 1 pitch

LOCATION: 🚗

Lost Horse Area
Rock Garden Valley Parking

SUN / SHADE:

AM ☀ | PM ☀ | ASPECT **S**

APPROACH: *Class 2*

Allow 15 minutes for a scramble up a boulder field. See the approach for **Freeway Wall** and **Tiny Tots Rock**.

Cake Walk is the second prominent crack on the upper wall. This route is identifiable by the fact that the crack rises vertically, and then traverses horizontally left before continuing upward toward the finish of the route.

EQUIPMENT: Standard Rack.

UPPER BELAY: Create Your Own.

DESCENT: *Class 3*

Walk back away from the climb to a short left-facing ramp. Down climb the ramp and turn right to scramble down a gully that takes you down to a notch. Turn right at the notch and work your way down and around back toward the start of the route.

GENERAL INFORMATION: This is one of the finest 5.9 climbs in the Park (another is Colorado Crack). It comes complete with a wide stem across a somewhat blank horizontal section. The fun continues as the route goes vertical after the traverse. Because of the somewhat "Z" nature of the route, you will probably experience some unwanted rope drag. Using two ropes may help avoid this problem. The route takes excellent protection. You can easily combine this route with Dinkey Doinks (5.8), which is located on the opposite wall. Have fun!

ROUTE DESCRIPTION: The start of the route follows the excellent vertical crack for approximately 30 feet (9 m) where it begins the short horizontal traverse. Starting the traverse can be a tricky proposition. You may need to climb above the traverse to get the protection you desire.

Traverse left for approximately 20 feet (6 m), stemming across a fairly blank section where you will be looking for the crux hand hold (which seems to be just out of reach). There are some good foot holds in this section that your feet will be happy to find.

After the traverse, the route has an awkward move as it follows the vertical portion of the route up toward the finish. You still have a few harder moves to make before you come to a respectable resting place. After this, the route eases up as you make the final moves to the top.

ROUTE NOTES:

Date Climbed: Led By:

Climbing Partners:

ROUTE 6

DiNKEY DOiNKS

DIFFICULTY: 5.8/ 1 pitch

LOCATION:

Lost Horse area
Rock Garden Valley Parking

SUN / SHADE:

AM	PM	ASPECT
☀	■	NE

APPROACH: *Class 2*
Allow 15 minutes for a scramble up a boulder field. See the approach for **Freeway Wall** and **Tiny Tots Rock**.

EQUIPMENT: Standard Rack.

UPPER BELAY: Create your own.

DESCENT: *Class 4*
Walk back away from the route and work your way left down through a 4th class down climb to a notch. Some climbers may want a "spot" or be lowered down one short, steep section of the down-climb. Since there is no rappel anchor located at the top of the climb, the last climber must be competent in down climbing 4th class unroped. Follow the notch back toward the start of the route.

The down climb is not as bad as it sounds but requires due diligence.

Dinkey Doinks

GENERAL INFORMATION: This route is a fun climb. You won't see other climbers here very often, so it can be a good alternative climb for busy weekends. You can easily combine this route with Cake Walk (5.9), which is located on the opposite wall or Beck's Bet (5.8) and Double Dogleg (5.7) which are located on the Shorter Wall.

ROUTE DESCRIPTION: This route provides classic crack climbing at the 5.8 level. Follow the crack as it climbs up to the top of the route with just a short jog to the left near the top of the climb. Protection possibilities are frequent and secure.

ROUTE NOTES:

Date Climbed: Led By:

Climbing Partners:

LOST HORSE AREA

ROUTE **7**

YOUNG LUST

DIFFICULTY: 5.9/ 1 pitch

LOCATION:

Lost Horse Area
Rock Garden Valley Parking

SUN / SHADE:

APPROACH: *Class 2*
Allow 30 minutes for a scramble through the boulders. See the approach for the "upper" **Shorter Wall**.

Go past the obvious "Double Dogleg" route. Your route is approximately 10 feet (3 m) left of Smithereens and is the second major crack on the face just left of the prominent wide crack.

EQUIPMENT: Standard Rack.

UPPER BELAY: Create Your Own.

DESCENT: *Rappel*
Rappel anchor at top of formation.

GENERAL INFORMATION: Young Lust! Brings back some fond memories. We were amazed the first time we scrambled up to this area. Never expected to see trees and grass up here. A real "Oasis". Sorry, no camels allowed.

Consider combining this route with Smithereens (5.9), Double Dogleg (5.7) or Beck's Bet (5.8).

ROUTE DESCRIPTION: This route earns and deserves its 5.9 rating, and you'll earn a couple of "stars" for sending it. The climbing is sustained but the protection placement opportunities are good. This is one of the best climbs on the wall.

Work up through the broken lower portion of the climb and continue to follow the crack to the top. No tricks, just treats here.

Climber on Young Lust

ROUTE NOTES:

Date Climbed: Led By:

Climbing Partners:

ROUTE 8

SMITHEREENS

DIFFICULTY: 5.9 / 1 pitch

LOCATION:

Lost Horse Area
Rock Garden Valley Parking

SUN / SHADE:

AM	PM	ASPECT
		N

APPROACH: *Class 2*

Allow 30 minutes for a scramble through the boulders. See the approach for the "upper" **Shorter Wall**.

Go past the obvious "Double Dogleg" route. Your route is approximately 10 feet (3 m) right of Young Lust and is the first major crack on the face just left of the prominent wide crack.

EQUIPMENT: Standard Rack.

UPPER BELAY: Create your own.

DESCENT: *Rappel*

Rappel anchor at top of formation.

GENERAL INFORMATION: Consider combining this route with Young Lust (5.9), Double Dogleg (5.7) or Beck's Bet (5.8).

ROUTE DESCRIPTION: Follow this crack as it heads up through a broken section before curving left to finish its journey to the top. Place plenty of protection on this route, as some holds have been known to break off, sending the climber on an unwanted journey!

Ocatillo

ROUTE NOTES:

Date Climbed: Led By:

Climbing Partners:

ROUTE 9

DIFFICULTY: 5.7 / 1 pitch

LOCATION:

Lost Horse Area
Rock Garden Valley Parking

SUN / SHADE:

AM	PM	ASPECT
■	■	N

APPROACH: *Class 2*
Allow 30 minutes for a scramble up through the boulders. See the approach for the "upper" **Shorter Wall.** Your route is the prominent dogleg crack in the middle of the face.

EQUIPMENT: Standard Rack.

UPPER BELAY: Bolts at the top of the route.

DESCENT: *Rappel*
Rappel anchor at top of formation, down and to the right of the top of Double Dogleg.

GENERAL INFORMATION: This route alone will make you glad you came to the Park to climb! The climbing never gets too difficult for 5.7. There are plenty of opportunities to place protection.

   If this route is occupied, consider climbing either Beck's Bet (5.8) to the right or Young Lust (5.9) and Smithereens (5.9) about 100 feet (30 m) to the left.

ROUTE DESCRIPTION: Climb up from the base of the route to the dogleg. Traverse slightly right using some fine footholds on the face for balance. Once past the right dogleg, the route swings back to the left to become an enjoyable hand crack the remaining distance to the top.

Scoping out Double Dogleg

ROUTE NOTES:

Date Climbed:	Led By:
Climbing Partners:	

ROUTE 10

BECK'S BET

DIFFICULTY: 5.8 / 1 pitch

LOCATION:

Lost Horse Area
Rock Garden Valley Parking

SUN / SHADE:

AM	PM	ASPECT
⬛	⬛	N

APPROACH: *Class 2*
Allow 30 minutes for a scramble through the boulders. See the approach for the "upper" **Shorter Wall**.

EQUIPMENT: Standard Rack.

UPPER BELAY: Belay from rappel anchor located up and to the left of the finish.

DESCENT: *Rappel*
Rappel anchor at top of formation.

GENERAL INFORMATION: This is a fun route and an excellent opportunity to improve your crack climbing technique. Consider combining this route with Double Dogleg (5.7) and Young Lust (5.9) for a "hat trick".

ROUTE DESCRIPTION: This is a straightforward vertical crack climb. There are no trick moves. Just get those hands in the crack until they hurt and start working your way up the route. Pain is your friend! You get a rest stop about half-way up the route on a nice ledge. Leaving a long sling on the last piece you place just below the ledge will mitigate rope drag.

Dave Cooper watches Charlie on lead.

ROUTE NOTES:

Date Climbed: _____ Led By: _____

Climbing Partners: _____

ROUTE 11

MR. MICHAEL GOES TO WASHINGTON

DIFFICULTY: 5.8 /1 pitch

LOCATION:

Lost Horse Area
Rock Garden Valley Parking

SUN / SHADE:

AM	PM	ASPECT
		NE

APPROACH: *Class 2*
Allow 10 minutes for an easy scramble through the boulders. See the approach for the "lower" **Shorter Wall.**

EQUIPMENT: Standard Rack.

UPPER BELAY: Create your own.

DESCENT: *Rappel*
Rappel anchors are located at the right end of the formation as you face the route.

GENERAL INFORMATION:
If this route is occupied, consider climbing either Double Dogleg (5.7), Beck's Bet (5.8) or Young Lust (5.9) up to your left on the "upper" Shorter Wall.

ROUTE DESCRIPTION:
Follow the crack that starts near the left side of the face as it goes up right to a vertical segment and then angles back to the left through a very thin section for a straight-up finish. The first few moves are somewhat difficult to protect.

View from Shorter Wall

ROUTE NOTES:.

Date Climbed: _____ Led By: _____

Climbing Partners: _____

LOST HORSE AREA

ROUTE 12

THE SWIFT

DIFFICULTY: 5.7 / 3 pitches

SUN / SHADE:

LOCATION: 🚗 D

Lost Horse Area
Lost Horse Wall Parking

APPROACH: *Class 2*
Allow 10 minutes to walk up a wash followed by easy scrambling. See the approach to **Lost Horse Wall**. This climb starts near a bush well to the left of the "black circle" seen about halfway up the wall.

EQUIPMENT: Pro to 3".

UPPER BELAY:
1st pitch: Create your own. Belay the first pitch on the prominent ledge just below the main vertical crack and to the right of the protruding boulder. This will reduce rope drag for the next pitch.
2nd pitch: Create your own. Belay from a platform of jumbled rocks prior to ascending into a corner and up a slab.
3rd pitch: Create your own. Belay in a convenient position at the top of the climb.

DESCENT: *Class 3*
Down climb along the top of the formation to your right as you face the route. Scramble right while gradually working your way down to a large dead tree and then move down toward another dead tree. From this point, you can scramble down to the ground and back around toward the start of the route.

GENERAL INFORMATION: A popular climb, especially on weekends. This is one of the few moderate multi-pitch routes in the Park. You may elect to do this route in 2 pitches, but rope drag might really become a "drag". Consider combining this route with Dappled Mare (5.8).

ROUTE DESCRIPTION: Start behind bushes to climb up to the prominent ledge and traverse right to a point just to the right of a boulder that juts out over most of the ledge. Belay here. Leave the ledge and climb the right hand of the two cracks that lead to the upper portion of the wall. Continue up and traverse diagonally to a point where the crack heads straight up to the corner for the belay.

Leave the belay stance and climb up slabs to a point below where further progress is blocked by a steeper section in front of you. Turn and climb up the wall to your right to gain the crack that continues up toward the top of the route. This section is probably the crux of the climb and can at first seem intimidating. A series of solid hand jams and stem moves will see you safely through this section. Continue up to a suitable belay stance at the top of the wall.

ROUTE NOTES:

Date Climbed: ___ Led By: ___

Climbing Partners: ___

LOST HORSE AREA

ROUTE 13

DAPPLED MARE

DIFFICULTY: 5.8 / 3 pitches

LOCATION: [D]

Lost Horse Area
Lost Horse Wall Parking

SUN / SHADE:

APPROACH: *Class 2*

Allow 10 minutes to walk up a wash followed by easy scrambling. See the approach to **Lost Horse Wall**. This route starts from a flat rock seen about halfway up the wall, well to the right of the "black circle".

EQUIPMENT: Standard Rack

UPPER BELAY:

1st pitch: Create your own. Belay from the prominent ledge at a point below the bottom of the main crack. This will reduce rope drag for the next pitch.
2nd pitch: Belay from bolts.
3rd pitch: Create your own at the top of the route.

DESCENT: *Class 3*

Down climb along the top of the formation to your right as you face the route. Scramble right while gradually working your way down to a large dead tree and then move down toward another dead tree. From this point you can scramble down to the ground and back around toward the start of the route.

GENERAL INFORMATION: This area is always popular with climbers. Weekends can be especially crowded. This is one of the few moderate multi-pitch routes in the Park. Another of those "must do" routes. Get up early; it's guaranteed to please. Roan Way is a variation for the top pitch that continues straight up from the point where you would normally make the short diagonal down climb from the bolts. Consider combining this route with The Swift (5.7).

ROUTE DESCRIPTION: Work your way up to the prominent ledge and then traverse right to the bottom of the main crack. Belay here. Follow the crack up to the bolts for the second pitch belay stance.

Traverse diagonally left and slightly down for a short distance to a point where the crack continues up vertically to the top of the route. If you leave the bolts and continue straight up, you will be doing the Roan Way (5.8) finish to the climb.

ROUTE NOTES:

Date Climbed: Led By:

Climbing Partners:

ROUTE 14

SOLAR TECHNOLOGY

DIFFICULTY: 5.6 / 1 pitch

LOCATION:

Lost Horse Area
Atlantis Area Parking

SUN / SHADE:

APPROACH: *Class 1*

Allow 10 minutes walking on trail. See the approach for **Atlantis Wall**.

This route is located about two-thirds of the way toward the right end of the wall and can be identified by the small dark colored patina at the very bottom of the climb.

EQUIPMENT: Standard Rack.

UPPER BELAY: Create your own.

DESCENT: *Class 2*

Walk off left as you face the route and down climb between the parallel walls. Once on the ground, circle back left to rejoin the trail back to the start of the route.

GENERAL INFORMATION: This area can be very crowded on hot sunny days due to being in the shade later in the day. Also, school groups frequent the area as it is easy to set up a series of top rope climbs.

ROUTE DESCRIPTION: Start up the route and follow the crack as it rises vertically up the face for a short stretch (the same start as for Men With Cow's Heads) and then angles left to finish. This is a fun lower grade route. The crack off to your right is Men With Cow's Heads (5.5).

Joshua Tree sunset

ROUTE NOTES:

Date Climbed: Led By:

Climbing Partners:

ROUTE 15

MEN WITH COW'S HEADS

DIFFICULTY: 5.5 / 1 pitch

SUN / SHADE:

LOCATION: E

Lost Horse Area
Atlantis Area Parking

APPROACH: *Class 1*

Allow 10 minutes walking on trail. See the approach for **Atlantis Wall**.

This route is located about two-thirds of the way toward the right end of the wall and can be identified by the small dark colored patina at the very bottom of the climb.

EQUIPMENT: Standard Rack.

UPPER BELAY: Create your own.

DESCENT: *Class 2*

Walk off left as you face the route and down climb between the parallel walls. Once on the ground, circle back left to rejoin the trail back to the start of the route.

GENERAL INFORMATION:

This area can be very crowded on hot sunny days due to being in the shade later in the day. Also, school groups frequent the area as it is easy to set up a series of top rope climbs.

Cholla cacti

ROUTE DESCRIPTION: Start up the route and follow the crack as it rises vertically up the face through broken sections of rock. This is a fun lower grade route.

The crack that angles off to your left after the first few moves is Solar Technology (5.6).

ROUTE NOTES:

Date Climbed: Led By:

Climbing Partners:

ROUTE 16

CLASSIC CORNER/FALSE CLASSIC CORNER

DIFFICULTY: 5.7 / 1 pitch

LOCATION:

Lost Horse Area
Atlantis Area Parking

SUN / SHADE:

Bonus Climb! False
Classic Corner

APPROACH: *Class 2*
Allow 25 minutes walking on trails plus a scramble up boulders. See the approach for **Cockroach Crag** in the Atlantis area.

EQUIPMENT: Pro to 3.5".

UPPER BELAY: Create your own.

DESCENT: *Class 4*
Climb toward the back of the formation away from the route and bear right to a point where you get to the top of a narrow split in the rocks. This is the "slot" mentioned in the General Information section. Ease your way down through this narrow slot to a series of ramps which are followed back to the beginning of the routes.

An easier, but longer, down climb exists off the left side of the formation. To descend this route, locate the obvious ramp which heads down away from the start of the climb. Follow this ramp to its conclusion and then scramble back to your left (toward the trail) through various boulders. This down climb brings you to the bottom of the formation after which you will need to work your way back around to the start of the routes by ascending the talus field.

GENERAL INFORMATION: These routes are off the beaten path, but fun. Standing at the base of the climbs, look up to your right to an area along the face with some Yuccas growing along the way. You should spot a "slot" on the horizon; this is the descent route which you will be need to locate after completing the climbs.

A fine dihedral crack climb called False Classic Corner lies around the block to the left of Classic Corner, and is probably rated 5.8.

ROUTE DESCRIPTION: Classic Corner works its way up a right-facing dihedral with various helpful features on both walls. Reach up past the wide triangular hole for a high hand-jam and step up into the horizontal crack to go for the finish.

On False Classic Corner, work your way up the crack to a point just below the roof. A layback/hand jam move will get you out from under the roof and back into the main crack. A series of strenuous hand jams combined with some welcomed face features will get you through this final section. You'll be glad you had your Wheaties™ for breakfast on this one!

ROUTE NOTES:

Date Climbed: _____ Led By: _____

Climbing Partners: _____

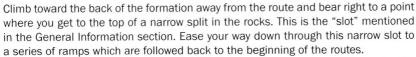

LOST HORSE AREA

ROUTE (17)

DR. SEUSS VOGEL

DIFFICULTY: 5.6 / 2 pitches

SUN / SHADE:

AM	PM	ASPECT
■	■	**N**

LOCATION: 🚗 **E**

Lost Horse Area
Atlantis Area Parking

APPROACH: *Class 1*
Allow 25 minutes walking on trails. See the approach for **Mt. Grossvogel**.

EQUIPMENT: Pro to 3".

UPPER BELAY: Create your own.

DESCENT: *Class 2*
Down climb to your right through boulders as you face the route.

The Aiguille de Joshua Tree

GENERAL INFORMATION: This route is off the beaten path but is a worthwhile, fun climb. Suppress the temptation to climb the Aiguille de Joshua Tree as it is "X" rated - you fall, maybe you die.

It is unlikely you'll see other climbers here, so it can be a good alternative area during busy weekends. The walk over to the climb is great for those cool mornings.

ROUTE DESCRIPTION: The route follows a crack up, then traverses left across and over a bulging feature. Once on easier ground, move back to the right and follow the crack as it goes up through a series of boulders to the top. Select a belay spot in the boulder section for bringing up your second.

ROUTE NOTES:

Date Climbed: Led By:

Climbing Partners:

ROUTE

ROBORANGER

DIFFICULTY: 5.5 / 2 pitches

SUN / SHADE:

AM	PM	ASPECT
■	■	N

LOCATION: 🚗 E

Lost Horse Area
Atlantis Area Parking

APPROACH: *Class 1*
Allow 25 minutes walking on trails. See the approach for **Mt. Grossvogel.**

EQUIPMENT: Pro to 3.5".

UPPER BELAY: Create your own.

DESCENT: *Class 2*
Down climb off to your right through boulders as you face the route.

GENERAL INFORMATION: This route is off the beaten path but is a worthwhile, fun climb. Suppress the temptation to climb the Aiguille de Joshua Tree as it is "X"rated - you fall, maybe you die.

It is unlikely you'll see other climbers here so it can be a good alternative formation during busy weekends. The walk over to the climb is great for those cool mornings.

ROUTE DESCRIPTION: Start on the right side of the detached block at the bottom of the route. Work up left to the crack that starts at the upper portion of the detached block. The roof is easily surmounted using a layback. Continue to follow the crack up to a minor platform, where you can set up a belay to avoid rope drag in the final section. Leave the belay and go left to finish the dihedral.

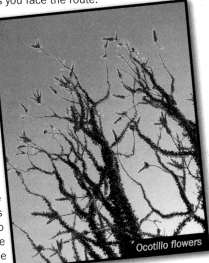
Ocotillo flowers

ROUTE NOTES:

Date Climbed:	Led By:
Climbing Partners:	

ROUTE

BECK'S BEAR

DIFFICULTY: 5.7 / 1 pitch

SUN / SHADE:

LOCATION: F2

Lost Horse Area
Park Boulevard - Hemingway Parking

APPROACH: *Class 1*
Allow 5 minutes for the approach. Follow the trail over to the formation. Head over to the tallest tree located next to the wall.

EQUIPMENT: Pro to 3.5".

UPPER BELAY: Create your own.

DESCENT: *Class 3*
Scramble off to your left as you face the route to the broken area of the wall. Down climb through the boulders back to the base of the climb.

GENERAL INFORMATION: Pro placement in the lower portion of the route can be a little tricky. Consider combining this route with Practice Rehearsal (5.7).

ROUTE DESCRIPTION: Start up a crack just behind a large pine tree. Some fun and somewhat committing moves lead you up to an easy finish.

ROUTE NOTES:

Date Climbed: Led By:

Climbing Partners:

Spring flowers

LOST HORSE AREA

ROUTE 20

PRACTICE REHEARSAL

DIFFICULTY: 5.7 / 1 pitch

LOCATION: F2

Lost Horse Area
Park Boulevard - Hemingway Parking

SUN / SHADE:

AM PM ASPECT NE

APPROACH: *Class 1*
Allow 5 minutes of easy walking on a trail over to the formation.

EQUIPMENT: Standard Rack.

UPPER BELAY: Create your own.

DESCENT: *Class 3*
Scramble off to your left as you face the route to the broken area of the wall. Down climb through the boulders back to the base of the climb.

GENERAL INFORMATION: Here's a fun route to do as a warm up or if the Dairy Queen Wall and Hemingway Wall are congested (as they can be on weekends).

This route might be a bit easier than its 5.7 rating indicates.

ROUTE DESCRIPTION: Climb up to the left of the slab past a small roof area, which is on your right, to a point where you are even with the other roof at the top of the slab. Follow the crack as it meanders up the face past a small bush and traverse slightly right to finish up on an arête. A variation can be done by continuing up a crack near the bush that leads diagonally to the left.

J-Tree and shadow

ROUTE NOTES:

Date Climbed: Led By:

Climbing Partners:

ROUTE 21

SCRUMDILLYISHUS

DIFFICULTY: 5.7 / 1 pitch

LOCATION:

Lost Horse Area
Park Boulevard - Hemingway Parking

SUN / SHADE:

AM	PM	ASPECT
		NE

APPROACH: *Class 2*
Allow 15 minutes of easy walking on a good trail followed by a scramble up some boulders. See the approach for **Dairy Queen Wall**.

EQUIPMENT: Pro to 3.5".

UPPER BELAY: Create your own.

DESCENT: *Rappel*
Rappel chains are located to the right of the top of this climb.

GENERAL INFORMATION: This route, along with Frosty Cone (5.7) and Mr. Misty Kiss (5.8), are definite "must do" routes.

This area is very popular and sees a lot of traffic, especially on weekends. If you really want to do routes in this area, we suggest that you get an early start. You will have a good idea as to route availability from the parking area. If the Dairy Queen Wall looks busy, you can head to the left and explore routes on Playhouse Rock or to the right to the Hemingway Wall. Both of these are visible from the parking area.

Dairy Queen rappel chains

ROUTE DESCRIPTION: Drop down into a narrow slot to start the climb, then follow the crack up to the point where it splits. Take the left-hand branch and head up toward a small alcove. Leave the alcove and follow the left crack to the top of the route where it becomes a little thinner. Protects well.

ROUTE NOTES:

Date Climbed: Led By:

Climbing Partners:

LOST HORSE AREA

ROUTE 22

FROSTY CONE

DIFFICULTY: 5.7 / 1 pitch

LOCATION:

Lost Horse Area
Park Boulevard - Hemingway Parking

SUN / SHADE:

  NE

APPROACH: *Class 2*
Allow 15 minutes of easy walking on good trail followed by a scramble up some boulders. See the approach for **Dairy Queen Wall**.

EQUIPMENT: Pro to 3.5".

UPPER BELAY: Create your own.

DESCENT: *Rappel*
Rappel chains are located to the right of the top of this climb.

GENERAL INFORMATION: This area is very popular and sees a lot of traffic, especially on weekends. If you really want to do routes in this area we suggest that you get an early start. You will have a good idea as to route availability from the parking area. If the Dairy Queen Wall looks busy you can head to the left and explore routes on Playhouse Rock or to the right for Hemingway Wall. Both of these are visible from the parking area.

ROUTE DESCRIPTION: Drop down into a narrow slot to start the climb, then follow the crack up to the point where it starts to split. Keep right and follow the crack up through solid holds to the broken area at the top of the climb. Good protection possibilities.

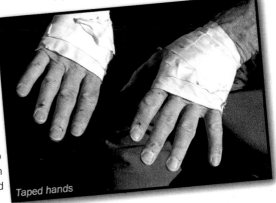
Taped hands

ROUTE NOTES:

Date Climbed:	Led By:
Climbing Partners:	

LOST HORSE AREA

ROUTE 23

MR. MISTY KISS

DIFFICULTY: 5.8 / 1 pitch

LOCATION: F1

Lost Horse Area
Park Boulevard - Hemingway Parking

SUN / SHADE:

AM	PM	ASPECT
◐	■	NE

APPROACH: *Class 2*
Allow 15 minutes of easy walking on a good trail followed by a scramble up some boulders. See the approach for **Dairy Queen Wall**.

EQUIPMENT: Standard Rack.

UPPER BELAY: Create your own.

DESCENT: *Rappel*
Rappel chains are located to the left of the top of this climb.

GENERAL INFORMATION: This route, along with Scrumdillyishus (5.7) and Frosty Cone (5.7), are definite "must do" routes.

This area is very popular and sees a lot of traffic, especially on weekends. If you really want to do routes in this area, we suggest that you get an early start. You will have a good idea as to route availability from the parking area. If the Dairy Queen Wall looks busy you can head to the left and explore routes on Playhouse Rock or to the right for the Hemingway Wall. Both of these are visible from the parking area.

Joshua tree and spring sky

ROUTE DESCRIPTION: Scramble up some large boulders by the base of the wall to start the climb, then follow the crack as it heads up and slants slightly left up to the top. No surprises here, just your basic, enjoyable crack climbing. Route has good protection possibilities.

ROUTE NOTES:

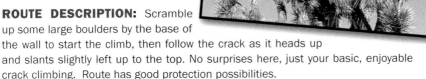

Date Climbed: Led By:

Climbing Partners:

ROUTE

DIFFICULTY: 5.9 / 1 pitch

SUN / SHADE:

LOCATION:

Lost Horse Area
Park Boulevard - Hemingway Parking

APPROACH: *Class 2*
Allow 15 minutes of easy walking on a good trail followed by a scramble up some boulders. See the approach for **Hemingway Buttress.**

EQUIPMENT: 1 or 2 ropes (see rappel options).

UPPER BELAY: Create your own.

DESCENT: *Rappel (1 or 2 ropes)*
2 Ropes: Rappel from chains to the right of White Lightning.
1 Rope: Rappel from an anchor located 25 yards/meters to the right of the 2 rope rappel

GENERAL INFORMATION: A challenging and exciting climb that will keep your interest from start to finish.

If this route is occupied, you are close to Dung Fu (5.7), Feltoneon Physics (5.8) and the always enjoyable White Lightning (5.7).

ROUTE DESCRIPTION: Work your way up to the prominent roof by climbing through a flakey area in the center of the route up toward two parallel cracks that lead up to the roof area. Once at the roof, angle up and right to the shoulder just left of Dung Fu. Follow a line that takes you up to what may be the crux of the climb, a challenging traverse to the left which intersects with the vertical crack which takes you to the top. A climb not to be missed!

Prickly pear in bloom

ROUTE NOTES:

Date Climbed: Led By:

Climbing Partners:

LOST HORSE AREA

ROUTE 25

DUNG FU

DIFFICULTY: 5.7 / 1 pitch

LOCATION:

SUN / SHADE:

Lost Horse Area
Park Boulevard - Hemingway Parking

APPROACH: *Class 2*
Allow 15 minutes of easy walking on a good trail followed by a scramble up some boulders. See the approach for **Hemingway Buttress**.

EQUIPMENT: 1 or 2 ropes (see rappel options). Pro to 3.5"

UPPER BELAY: Create your own.

DESCENT: *Rappel (1 or 2 ropes)*
2 Ropes: Rappel from chains to the right of White Lightning.
1 Rope: Rappel from an anchor located 25 yards/meters to the right of the 2 rope rappel.

GENERAL INFORMATION: This is an interesting route in many ways. It starts out as your basic dihedral crack climb and then goes subterranean about half way up the route. You head back into a cave where a series of chimney moves lead you to the top. Some of our friends refuse to lead (or follow) this route due to the cave moves (or perhaps it's the bat droppings in the back of the cave). Is "Dung Fu" a messy variation of Kung Fu? Don't climb this one if you can't take a joke!

This route may be split into 2 pitches for less rope-drag.

ROUTE DESCRIPTION: The route starts off up a standard hand crack and follows a right facing dihedral on its way up to the cave area. You will find a good selection of hand holds on the left face of the climb on your way up. Squeeze your way into the opening of the roomy "cave" where you may wish to set up a belay for a first pitch using some cams/stoppers for protection. It is possible to climb the route as a single pitch.

Climb out of the cave by doing a few chimney moves, which are well protected by placements in the crack in the back and top of the cave. Leave the cave and chimney area behind as you climb back into the sunlight, traversing over a small tree on the face for a finish to the climb.

ROUTE NOTES:

Date Climbed:	Led By:
Climbing Partners:	

ROUTE 26

DIFFICULTY: 5.7 / 1 pitch

LOCATION: F1

Lost Horse Area
Park Boulevard - Hemingway Parking

SUN / SHADE:
AM PM ASPECT
NE

APPROACH: *Class 2*
Allow 15 minutes of easy walking on a good trail followed by a scramble up some boulders. See the approach for **Hemingway Buttress**.

EQUIPMENT: 1 or 2 ropes (see rappel options). Pro to 3".

UPPER BELAY: Create your own.

DESCENT: *Rappel (1 or 2 ropes)*
2 Ropes: Rappel from chains to the right of White Lightning.
1 Rope: Rappel from an anchor located 25 yards/meters to the right of the 2 rope rappel.

On White Lightning

GENERAL INFORMATION: Due to its solid 5.7 rating, this route is one of the most popular in the Park and understandably one of the first 5.7 routes for many climbers. It is always a joy to lead and plenty of fun to follow. If this route is occupied, you are close to the unusual Dung Fu (5.7), Feltoneon Physics (5.8) and the always-challenging Overseer (5.9).

ROUTE DESCRIPTION: The major difficulties on this route lie near the bottom in the form of a very strenuous off-width section. There is a convenient handhold located near the back of the crack just below the minor roof which will give you some purchase on the rock while you negotiate this area. After passing this section the climbing becomes easier with plenty of opportunities for protection. Up you go!

The 5.7 route finishes off to the left near the top. Going right involves some 5.9+ climbing.

ROUTE NOTES:

Date Climbed: _____   Led By: _____

Climbing Partners: _____

ROUTE 27

FELTONEON PHYSICS

DIFFICULTY: 5.8 / 1 pitch

LOCATION:

Lost Horse
Park Boulevard - Hemingway Parking

SUN / SHADE:

AM	PM	ASPECT
		NE

APPROACH: *Class 2*
Allow 15 minutes of easy walking on a good trail followed by a scramble up some boulders. See the approach for **Hemingway Buttress**.

EQUIPMENT: 1 or 2 ropes (see rappel options) Pro to 3".

UPPER BELAY: Create your own.

DESCENT: *Rappel (requires to ropes)*
2 Ropes: Rappel from chains to the right of White Lightning.
1 Rope: Rappel from an anchor located 25 yards/
meters to the right of the 2 rope rappel.

Desert flowers

GENERAL INFORMATION: If this route is occupied, you are close to the dreaded Dung Fu (5.7), the ever-appealing White Lightning (5.7), and the always-challenging Overseer (5.9).

ROUTE DESCRIPTION: Scramble up the right-sloping rock at the base of the climb to a move transitioning over into the right-facing crack. Ascend the short column to a vertical crack. Climb up to a point where the crack splits left and right. Traverse to your right to a vertical crack. Ascend the crack, and move right again to climb a gap between two boulders.

ROUTE NOTES:

Date Climbed: Led By:

Climbing Partners:

REAL HIDDEN VALLEY

28 Fote Hog
29 Count On Your Fingers
30 Butterfingers Make Me Horny
31 Almost Vertical
32 Ain't Nothing But A J-Tree Thing
33 Sail Away

⬤ 5.5 / 5.6   ⬛ 5.7

◼ 5.8   ◆ 5.9

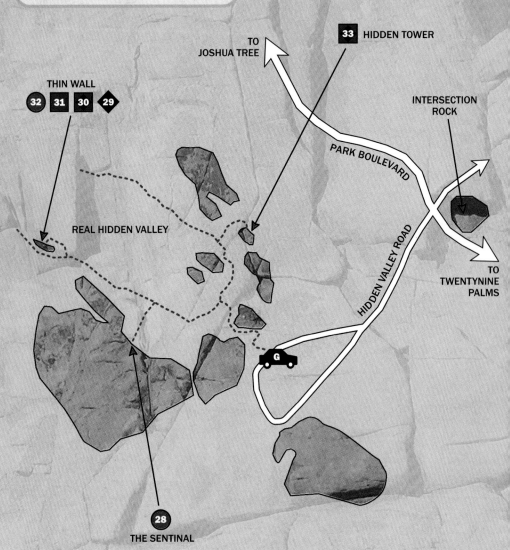

TO JOSHUA TREE

33 HIDDEN TOWER

THIN WALL
32 31 30 29

INTERSECTION ROCK

PARK BOULEVARD

REAL HIDDEN VALLEY

HIDDEN VALLEY ROAD

TO TWENTYNINE PALMS

G

28
THE SENTINAL

REAL HIDDEN VALLEY - ACCESS

PARKING: G

FORMATIONS: The Sentinel (for Route **28** Fote Hog)
Thin Wall (for Route **29** Count on your Fingers, Route **30** Butterfingers Make Me Horny,
Route **31** Almost Vertical, and Route **32** Ain't Nothing But a J-Tree Thing)
Hidden Tower (for Route **33** Sail Away).

LOCATION: From the intersection of Park Boulevard and Hidden Valley Picnic Area Road, follow the paved road to the parking area for the Hidden Valley Loop Trail.

Walk up the Hidden Valley Loop Trail for a short distance until you reach a "T" intersection as the valley opens in front of you. The popular Loop Trail will take you close to each of the formations in this area.

TO THE SENTINEL:
Approach: Class 1
At the "T" intersection turn left and follow the trail for less than 5 minutes until you are standing in front of a large face on your left. Fote Hog starts by ascending the vertical crack to the right of the small tree growing out of the left-slanting ramp.

TO THIN WALL:
Approach: Class 1
Allow ten minutes of easy walking. Turn left at the "T" intersection of the Hidden Valley Loop Trail and follow the trail for less than 5 minutes until you reach the far end of a large wall on your left (The Sentinel). The formation directly in front of you as you walk along the trail is the edge of the Thin Wall. Bear slightly right on a minor trail to reach the northeast face of the Thin Wall. **Please see the routes for Thin Wall on page 101.**

TO HIDDEN TOWER:
Approach: Class 2
Allow 10 minutes of easy walking followed by an easy scramble. Turn right at the "T" intersection of the Hidden Valley Loop Trail and follow the trail for about 5 minutes until you come to a tall formation on your right that we think resembles a giant "Hershey's Kiss", leave the trail here, to the right, and make your way through the boulders, circling around to the base of Hidden Tower (the taller formation on the right). As viewed from the loop trail Sail Away is on the back side of Hidden Tower.

Start of the Hidden Valley Loop Trail

The Sentinel watches over Hidden Valley

Thin Wall in the distance

The "Hershey's Kiss" formation

ROUTE 28

DIFFICULTY: 5.6 / 2 pitches

SUN / SHADE:

AM	PM	ASPECT
■	■	N

LOCATION:

Real Hidden Valley
Hidden Valley Loop Trail Parking

APPROACH: *Class 1*
Allow 5 minutes walking on a nature trail. See the approach to **The Sentinel**. Look for a small tree growing out of the center of a left-slanting ramp. This tree marks the start of Fote Hog.

EQUIPMENT: Standard Rack.

BELAY:
1st Pitch: Create your own. Belay from just above the flakes on the face.
2nd Pitch: Create your own. Belay from the top of the climb above the layback crack.

DESCENT: *Class 2*
Scramble off to your left as you face the climb.

Fote Hog detail

GENERAL INFORMATION: Because of rope drag, this climb is normally done as two pitches. It is a very interesting route that will keep you guessing. There's always a good hand/foot hold just when you need it. You don't want to pass this one up on your way to the Thin Wall.

ROUTE DESCRIPTION: Scramble up a left-sloping ramp to a small tree, which makes a good spot to set up a belay. Climb up past an inset triangle to a horizontal crack that appears just about the time you're beginning to wonder what to do. Traverse right to a good stance with a bomber handhold. The next move can really be exciting if you're short. Climb up by pulling up on a large knob to gain access to a knobby area, which leads to another ramp, where you can set up a belay. Angle up and right along the ramp passing a light, white colored rock and eventually reaching a left-facing dihedral. Continue up this fun dihedral to the finish of the climb.

ROUTE NOTES:

Date Climbed:	Led By:
Climbing Partners:	

REAL HIDDEN VALLEY

ROUTE 29

COUNT ON YOUR FINGERS

DIFFICULTY: 5.9 / 1 pitch

LOCATION:

Real Hidden Valley
Hidden Valley Loop Trail Parking

SUN / SHADE:

APPROACH: *Class 1*
Allow 10 minutes walking on a nature trail. See the approach to **Thin Wall**.

EQUIPMENT: Standard Rack.

UPPER BELAY: There are bolts at the top of the climb which can be used for the upper belay.

DESCENT: *Rappel*
Rappel from chains at the top of the route.

GENERAL INFORMATION: This is a very popular climbing area, especially with larger groups. Consider Sail Away (5.8) across the valley.

ROUTE DESCRIPTION: This route starts out moderate and gets progressively more difficult (especially if you're short) and finishes in the 5.9 section. There are numerous choices of where to climb and protect, but basically stay on the face and to the left of the edge. The last couple of moves at the top of the climb go easier in a crack to the right.
This is a great route, which is easy to protect. This is another of those "must do" routes. Try it, you'll like it!

Charlie leads Count Your Fingers

ROUTE NOTES:

Date Climbed: Led By:

Climbing Partners:

REAL HIDDEN VALLEY

ROUTE

BUTTERFINGERS MAKE ME HORNY

DIFFICULTY: 5.8 / 1 pitch

LOCATION:

Real Hidden Valley
Hidden Valley Loop Trail Parking

SUN / SHADE:

AM | PM | ASPECT
NE

APPROACH: *Class 1*
Allow 10 minutes walking on a nature trail. See the approach to **Thin Wall**.

EQUIPMENT: Standard Rack.

UPPER BELAY: Create your own.

DESCENT: *Class 3*
Scramble to your right as you face the route, up and over a series of boulders to the end of the formation, then work your way down to the ground.

GENERAL INFORMATION:
This is a very popular climbing area, especially with larger groups. Consider Sail Away (5.8) across the valley.

ROUTE DESCRIPTION:
Move up past a couple of small ledges until you can plug in some pro into a horizontal crack. Protection opportunities improve from this point upward, as you follow a vertical crack to the top. Stay to the left near the top of the climb, using the thinner crack rather than the wide crack that goes to the right.

Routes on Thin Wall

ROUTE NOTES:

Date Climbed: _____ Led By: _____

Climbing Partners: _____

REAL HIDDEN VALLEY

ROUTE **31**

ALMOST VERTICAL

DIFFICULTY: 5.7 / 1 pitch

SUN / SHADE:

LOCATION: **G**

Real Hidden Valley
Hidden Valley Loop Trail Parking

APPROACH: *Class 1*
Allow 10 minutes walking on a nature trail. See the approach to **Thin Wall**.

EQUIPMENT: Standard Rack.

UPPER BELAY: Create your own.

DESCENT: *Class 3*
Scramble to your right as you face the route, up and over a series of boulders to the end of the formation, then work your way down to the ground.

GENERAL INFORMATION: This is a very popular climbing area, especially with larger groups. Consider Sail Away (5.8) across the valley.

ROUTE DESCRIPTION: Scramble up the boulders to the ledge at the bottom of the climb. The climbing is straightforward and follows the vertical crack. Some people start this climb from the ground, climbing straight up through the boulders in front of the wall. There is more potential for rope drag with this start, and this start isn't as "aesthetically pleasing" as the vertical crack above.

Blooming Ocotillos

ROUTE NOTES:

Date Climbed:	Led By:
Climbing Partners:	

ROUTE 32

AIN'T NOTHING BUT A J-TREE THING

DIFFICULTY: 5.6 / 1 pitch

LOCATION:

SUN / SHADE:

AM	PM	ASPECT
☀	■	NE

Real Hidden Valley
Hidden Valley Loop Trail Parking

APPROACH: *Class 1*
Allow 10 minutes walking on a nature trail. See the approach to **Thin Wall**.

EQUIPMENT: Pro to 3".

UPPER BELAY: Create your own.

DESCENT: *Class 3*
Scramble to your right as you face the route, up and over a series of boulders to the end of the formation, then work your way down to the ground.

GENERAL INFORMATION: This is a very popular climbing area, especially with larger groups. Consider Sail Away (5.8) across the valley.

ROUTE DESCRIPTION: Scramble up the boulders to the ledge at the bottom of the climb. Climb the vertical crack and bear left at the "Y" near the top of the route.

J-Tree forest

ROUTE NOTES:

Date Climbed: _____ Led By: _____

Climbing Partners: _____

REAL HIDDEN VALLEY

ROUTE 33

SAIL AWAY

DIFFICULTY: 5.8 / 1 pitch

LOCATION:

Real Hidden Valley
Hidden Valley Loop Trail Parking

SUN / SHADE:

AM	PM	ASPECT
		N

APPROACH: *Class 2*

Allow 10 minutes of easy walking on a nature trail followed by an easy scramble. See the approach to **Hidden Tower**.

The route begins at ground level, requiring an easy scramble down among some boulders to the base of the tower.

EQUIPMENT: Standard Rack.

UPPER BELAY: Belay from the rappel anchor.

DESCENT: *Rappel*

Rappel anchor at top of route.

GENERAL INFORMATION: This is one of the most popular climbs in the Park, and one of our favorites. Plan on climbing an alternate route in this same area if it looks like it will be a while before you can get on the route. Suggestion: Thin Wall climbs.

ROUTE DESCRIPTION: Belay the lead climber from the ground down among the boulders. Start the climb from this spot for more of a challenge. If you prefer an easier start, you can begin by scrambling up the boulders to the right, and stepping across to a small ledge. We hope you'll just "sail" through this climb.

From the ledge, follow the prominent crack up toward the top of the climb. Exit either left or right at the top to gain the anchor.

Leading Sail Away

REAL HIDDEN VALLEY

ROUTE NOTES:

Date Climbed: Led By:

Climbing Partners:

HIDDEN VALLEY CAMPGROUND AREA

34 Overhang Bypass   36 Toe Jam   38 The Bong
35 Double Cross   37 Buissonier   39 Hands Off

5.5 / 5.6   5.7   5.8

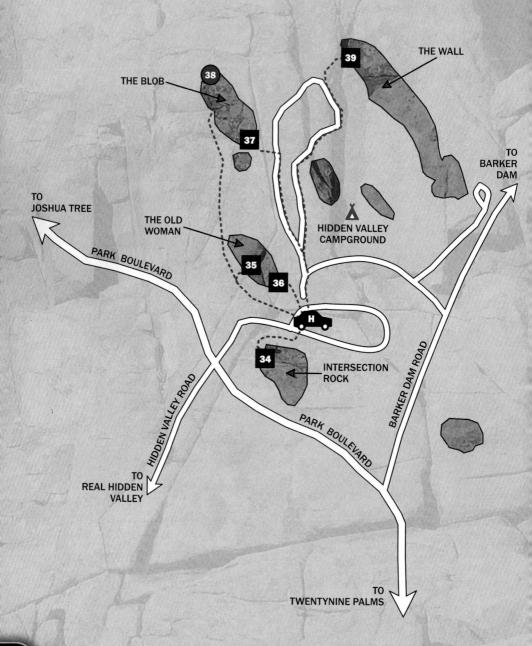

THE WALL

39

THE BLOB
38

37

TO
BARKER
DAM

TO
JOSHUA TREE

PARK BOULEVARD

THE OLD
WOMAN

HIDDEN VALLEY
CAMPGROUND

35

36

H

34

INTERSECTION
ROCK

HIDDEN VALLEY ROAD

BARKER DAM ROAD

TO
REAL HIDDEN
VALLEY

PARK BOULEVARD

TO
TWENTYNINE PALMS

108

HiDDEN VALLEY CAMPGROUND - ACCESS

PARKING:

FORMATIONS: Intersection Rock (for Route **34** Overhang Bypass),
The Old Woman (for Route **35** Double Cross, and Route **36** Toe Jam)
The Blob (for Route **37** Bussonier, and Route **38** The Bong)
The Wall (for Route **39** Hands off)

LOCATION: Drive to the intersection of Park Boulevard and the road to Hidden Valley picnic area. Instead of turning toward the Hidden Valley picnic area, turn the opposite direction to enter a large parking lot between Intersection Rock and the Hidden Valley Campground.

TO INTERSECTION ROCK:

Approach: Class 1
Intersection Rock is located immediately next to the parking lot - you drove past it as you entered the lot. Circle around slightly to the right of the formation to start Overhang Bypass.

Bypassing the overhang

Intersection Rock as seen from the parking lot. Overhang Bypass is easily seen in profile high on the right side of the formation.

Double Cross

The Old Woman

Toe Jam

The Bong (opposite side of formation)

Buissonier

The Blob

To Hands Off

The Old Woman and *The Blob* from the Intersection Rock parking lot.

*Climber on **Toe Jam***

TO THE OLD WOMAN:

Standing with your back to Intersection Rock, you'll see The Old Woman formation at about 10:00.

Approach: Class 1 (Double Cross)

Allow 5 minutes of walking along a trail. Head west on a trail from the parking area, circling around to the left side of The Old Woman. Walk approximately 100 feet (30 m) while paralleling Park Boulevard. Turn right and head to the base of the formation. The route is the obvious vertical crack with two prominent horizontal lines crossing it.

Approach: Class 1 (Toe Jam)

Allow 5 minutes to walk along a road and scramble up to the base of the climb. Walk north from the parking lot, past the restroom, then swing left, crossing between campsites # 29 and # 30 in Hidden Valley Campground.

TO THE BLOB:

Approach: Class 1 (Bussonier)

Allow 5 minutes for the approach for Bussonier. Walk past the restroom to the paved road for Hidden Valley Campground, and make your way toward campsite # 21.

Approach: Class 2 (The Bong)

Head west from the parking area, walking to the left of The Old Woman formation and passing in front of Double Cross. Follow the trail as it heads toward the next formation on your right - this is The Blob - South Face. Walk along parallel to The Blob until you see a prominent crack that runs up the full left end of the face. Scramble up toward the bottom of this crack to a dike which angles up to your left. Walk along the dike as it traverses the face and curves around right to the start of the climb.

Mai-Lan leading The Bong

Top of The Bong

Climb begins around corner

Approach

Hike around the south side of The Blob, then scramble up to an easy ramp to reach the base of The Bong.

TO THE WALL:

Approach: Class 1 (Bussonier)

Walk from the parking lot, past the restroom, and follow the paved Hidden Valley Campground road until you are between campsites #15 and #16. Turn right here, leaving the road and hiking up among some boulders to a tree at the base of the formation. Take care not to cut through any occupied campsite.

Hands Off

Hands Off is located near the north end of The Wall.

ROUTE 34

OVERHANG BYPASS

DIFFICULTY: 5.7 / 2 pitches

SUN / SHADE:

LOCATION:

Hidden Valley Campground Area
Intersection Rock Parking

APPROACH: *Class 1*
Allow 5 minutes of easy walking. Walk south from the parking lot, toward Intersection Route. Head around to the right of the base of the formation for about 30 yards. The route climbs up to the obvious roof on the formation in front of you.

EQUIPMENT: 1 or 2 ropes (see rappel options).

UPPER BELAY:
1st Pitch: Create your own anchor under the roof.
2nd Pitch: Bolts at the top of the formation.

DESCENT: *Rappel (1 or 2 ropes)*
Rappel from the anchor at the top of route toward the parking lot. Rappel down the north face to the right of the Ski Track routes. A single rope rappel takes you to a large ramp, which allows you to down climb toward the base of Overhang Bypass. Two ropes will allow you to rappel the entire distance back to the ground; practically right back to your parked vehicle!

GENERAL INFORMATION: This is a very popular route, which includes an exciting traverse under a roof. Study the formation carefully to decide which line you want to take on lead. There are several possible variations from which to choose for the first section of the climb.

ROUTE DESCRIPTION: Start up one of the lower ramps to the right of the route. Climb up toward the long horizontal crack located lower on the left face below a small cave. Climb past the horizontal crack into the cave. Traverse out to your left and follow a line which leads you up into the upper left end of the roof section. Belay from here.

    Finish the route by traversing under the roof to the right and onto the face where you will find a nice stance with a welcomed bolt for protection. Scramble up the slab above the bolt to the top of the formation. An anchor is located back away from the face you just climbed.

ROUTE NOTES:

Date Climbed:	Led By:
Climbing Partners:	

ROUTE 35

DOUBLE CROSS

DIFFICULTY: 5.8 / 1 pitch

LOCATION:

Hidden Valley Campground Area
Intersection Rock Parking

SUN / SHADE:

HiDDEN VALLEY CAMPGROUND AREA

APPROACH: *Class 1*
Allow 5 minutes of easy walking. See the approach to **The Old Woman (Double Cross)**.

EQUIPMENT: 1 or 2 ropes (see rappel options). Pro to 3.5".

UPPER BELAY: Belay from chains at the top of the route.

DESCENT: *Rappel (1 or 2 ropes)*
Rappel from chains at top of route. Take note that a single 60 meter rope will get you to a point where you can downclimb a steep ramp. Be sure to tie a knot at the ends of your rope so you don't accidentally rappel off the end!

GENERAL INFORMATION: An easy approach combined with a quality route make this one of the most popular routes in the Park, especially during the weekends. This route is often free soloed. It has also been the scene of numerous serious falls. Hopefully the meaning of the name "Double Cross" isn't synonymous with multiple deaths!

ROUTE DESCRIPTION: The route starts off on the lower right side of the crack. Scramble up and over to your left onto a small ledge about 15 feet (5 m) off the ground. You may be able to place protection in a horizontal crack just below the ledge on the right side of the climb. We also suggest placing one or two small, equalized TCU cams or stoppers in the horizontal crack left of the ledge at the start of the climb. This will help lock in your upper protection in the event of a fall.

The first couple of moves involve some very solid hand jamming just below what is probably the crux of the route, a bulging section of rock. Conventional wisdom along with conventional climbing wisdom (whatever that is) dictate that the leader place a couple of solid cams in this area.

Once past the bulge, progress involves straightforward crack climbing, using cams for protection. This climb takes "good" hands and feet. Don't pass up an opportunity to lead or follow this one. This is a classic, "must do" climb.

ROUTE NOTES:

Date Climbed: Led By:

Climbing Partners:

ROUTE 36

TOE JAM

DIFFICULTY: 5.7 / 1 pitch

LOCATION:

Hidden Valley Campground Area
Intersection Rock Parking

SUN / SHADE:

APPROACH: *Class 1*
Allow 5 minutes of easy walking. See the approach to **The Old Woman (Toe Jam)**. Cross between campsites # 29 and # 30 in Hidden Valley Campground and scramble up easy ramps to the start of the climb.

EQUIPMENT: Standard Rack.

UPPER BELAY: Create your own.

DESCENT: *Rappel*
Rappel anchor to the right of the top of the route.

GENERAL INFORMATION: It is not unusual to see a climbing party on this route. The short nature of the climb, its reasonable rating as well as its close proximity to parking and the campground all combine to make it a popular route. This is a fun route that can be used as a good warm up for some of the other area climbs, which include Double Cross (5.8), Overhang Bypass (5.7), and Hands Off (5.8)

ROUTE DESCRIPTION: Follow the crack as it curves up and to the right to join up with a crack system that goes up vertically to the top of the pitch.

Climber on Toe Jam

ROUTE NOTES:

Date Climbed: Led By:

Climbing Partners:

ROUTE 37

BUISSONIER

DIFFICULTY: 5.7 / 1 pitch

SUN / SHADE:

LOCATION:

Hidden Valley Campground Area
Intersection Rock Parking

APPROACH: *Class 1*
Allow 5 minutes of walking along a road followed by an easy scramble. See the
approach to **The Blob (Buissonier)**, using the approach through the campground.

This route is located behind campsite #21. Ask permission to climb the route if
this campsite is occupied. Walk around to the right side of the campsite, and work
your way back into a corridor, under a series of boulders to the start of the route.

EQUIPMENT: Standard Rack.

UPPER BELAY: Create your own.

DESCENT: *Rappel / Class 4*
If you choose to rappel, there is usually a rappel anchor built with slings, located
between boulders down and off to your right as you face the route. This rappel has
a tricky and awkward start. Examine the slings carefully before deciding to use them,
and be prepared to rebuild the rappel anchor entirely. It is possible to down climb by
traversing left from the top of the route to a chimney, which involves a few stemming
moves. You'll end up further back in the corridor where the climb began.

GENERAL INFORMATION: *Buissonier* is French for the name of a non-alcoholic
drink, a Western Scrub-Jay, and is very close to a French word for playing hooky from
school. Who knows what the person naming the route really had in mind? This route
will keep you guessing whether to try a lie-back move or to try to maneuver both feet
into the crack, so you may not be thinking about the translation as you climb.

ROUTE DESCRIPTION: Begin in a cozy opening between the Blob and various
large boulders just below the start of the crack. Chimney and/or stretch from on top
of a skinny rock into position behind a leaning boulder to reach the first thin holds
in the bottom of the crack

The route angles to the left then heads up more vertically through what is
possibly the crux. The angle eases up as you make your way to a flat area at the top.
A somewhat awkward route, but we guarantee you won't be bored. One friend
described this climb as "spicy"!

ROUTE NOTES:

Date Climbed: Led By:

Climbing Partners:

down climb

ROUTE

THE BONG

DIFFICULTY: 5.5 / 1 pitch

LOCATION:

Hidden Valley Campground Area
Intersection Rock Parking

SUN / SHADE:

APPROACH: *Class 2*
Allow 10 minutes for an easy hike and a short scramble. Leave the parking lot and swing to the left of **The Old Woman**, walking past **Double Cross** and over to the south face of **The Blob**. See the approach to **The Blob (The Bong)** for more details.

EQUIPMENT: Standard Rack.

UPPER BELAY: Create your own.

DESCENT: *Class 4*
Walk down to a ledge located off to your left as you face the route. Down climb the 4th class rock past a bush to a point where you are even with the corridor that leads over to the start of the route. Now comes the fun part.

Ease your way under the boulder, which partially blocks the corridor; feet first works best. Once you are in this passageway you can either perform some stemming or chimney moves to work your way back to the start of the route. Was that cool or what?

If the 4th class portion of the down climb intimidates your less experienced climbers, there is the option of setting up a belay for the down climb.

Mai-Lan on The Bong

GENERAL INFORMATION: This would be a good route on which to "cut your teeth" for leading. It reminds us of an easier version of Mental Physics. This is a fun route to do as a warm up.

ROUTE DESCRIPTION: Climb the crack. A small roof is surmounted by using a few convenient holds on the left side of the crack.

ROUTE NOTES:

Date Climbed:	Led By:
Climbing Partners:	

ROUTE 39

HANDS OFF

DIFFICULTY: 5.8 / 1 pitch

LOCATION:

Hidden Valley Campground Area
Intersection Rock Parking

SUN / SHADE:

APPROACH: *Class 1*
Allow 5 minutes walk from the parking area. See the approach to **The Wall**.
   Leave the road between campsites #15 and # 16. The route starts up on a small "bench" of rock behind a large tree.

EQUIPMENT: Standard Rack.

UPPER BELAY: Create your own.

DESCENT: *Class 2*
An easy walk off behind and to the left of the route as you face the formation.

GENERAL INFORMATION: An entertaining climb which, due to its location, sees a moderate number of ascents.

ROUTE DESCRIPTION: The start of this route is where the initial difficulty lies. An off-width, flaring crack forces you to reach out and around to the right. While protection is possible here, it is still a place you are happy to leave behind you.

Ocotillo bloom

   The remaining portion of the climb is rather straightforward until you come to a cruxy area about midway up. All in all, an enjoyable route where you can take pleasure in the misery of those who have to follow what you have led!

ROUTE NOTES:

Date Climbed:	Led By:
Climbing Partners:	

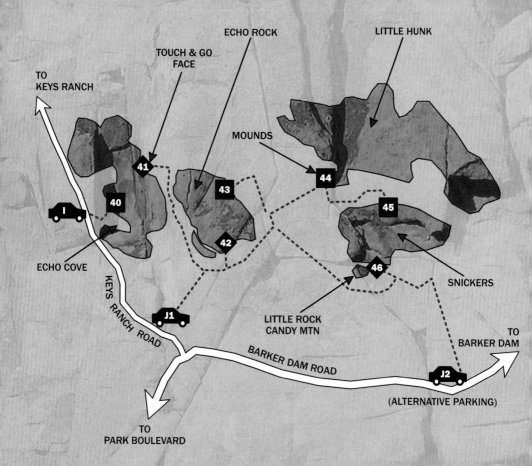

ECHO ROCK AREA

40 Fun Stuff
41 Touch And Go
42 Pope's Crack
43 Bambi Meets Godzilla
44 Eff Eight
45 Funny Bone
46 M & Ms Plain

 5.8   5.9

ECHO ROCK

LITTLE HUNK

TOUCH & GO
FACE

MOUNDS

TO
KEYS RANCH

41

44

45

40

43

42

46

ECHO COVE

SNICKERS

KEYS RANCH ROAD

J1

LITTLE ROCK
CANDY MTN

BARKER DAM ROAD

TO
BARKER DAM

J2

(ALTERNATIVE PARKING)

TO
PARK BOULEVARD

ECHO ROCK AREA - ACCESS

PARKING: I

FORMATIONS: **Echo Cove** (for Route **40** Fun Stuff)

LOCATION: From the intersection of Park Boulevard and Barker Dam Road, drive 1.3 miles (2.1 km) on Barker Dam Road to the intersection with the Keys Ranch Road. Turn left at this intersection and proceed on for 0.3 mile (0.5 km) on a dirt road toward the entry to Keys Ranch. Turn right into the fenced off dirt parking area.

Fun Stuff starts below the dark-colored rocks seen on the far left in this view.

TO ECHO COVE:
Approach: Class 1
Allow 5 minutes walking on a faint trail. Fun Stuff is on the left side of the "valley."

PARKING: J1

FORMATIONS: **Touch and Go Face** (for Route **41** Touch and Go)
Echo Rock (for Route **42** Pope's Crack, and Route **43** Bambi Meets Godzilla)
Mounds (for Route **44** Eff Eight)
Snickers (for Route **45** Funny Bone)
Little Rock Candy Mountain (for Route **46** M&M's Plain)

LOCATION: From the intersection of Park Boulevard and Barker Dam Road, drive 1.3 miles (2.1 km) on Barker Dam Road to its intersection with the Keys Ranch Road. Turn left at this intersection and turn into the large parking lot located immediately to your right.

TO TOUCH & GO FACE:
Approach: Class 2
Allow 10 minutes easy walking on a good trail, followed by a short scramble. Follow the marked trail to the left of the restroom as it leaves the parking area toward Echo Rock. Turn left when you encounter the wide wash. Follow the wash until near the end of Echo Rock which is on your right. Turn left here and scramble up through the boulders toward an obvious dihedral on the face. This is Touch and Go.

To Touch and Go

To Pope's Crack

Echo Rock

Head straight back along a wash and turn left to reach Touch & Go.

Touch & Go is the dramatic crack in the center of the photo.

Bambi Meets Godzilla

Eff Eight

Funny Bone

M & M's Plain

Echo Rock

Mounds

Snickers

View from the parking lot. **Pope's Crack** is just beyond the left edge of the photo.

Pope's Crack.

TO ECHO ROCK:

Echo Rock is the expansive formation with a huge domed face that dominates the view from the parking lot.

Approach: Class 2 (Pope's Crack)

Allow 10 minutes walking on good trails followed by an easy scramble. Follow the marked trail to the left of the restroom as it leaves the parking area toward Echo Rock. Turn right at a wash, and hike toward the right (east) end of Echo Rock. When you reach the end of Echo Rock, turn left and work your way up among some boulders to the start of the route. Pope's Crack is quite visible from the trail.

Approach: Class 1 (Bambi Meets Godzilla)

Allow 15 minutes walking on trails. Follow the marked trail to the left of the restroom as it leaves the parking lot toward Echo Rock. Turn right at a wash and hike to the right (east) end of Echo Rock. Circle around the end of Echo Rock to where the trail intersects another trail. Turn left here and hike for approximately 100 yards until you see the largest tree on this end of the face. The route begins directly behind the tallest tree at the base of the formation.

TO MOUNDS:

Approach: Class 1

Allow 15 minutes walking on trails. Follow the marked trail to the left of the restroom as it leaves the parking area toward Echo Rock. Turn right into a wash and hike around toward the right (east) end of Echo Rock. Look straight ahead; the prominent, lone crack on the small formation directly in front of you is Eff Eight.

Bambi Meets Godzilla

Head for the tall evergreen at the base of the wall to find out the fate of Bambi when she met Godzilla

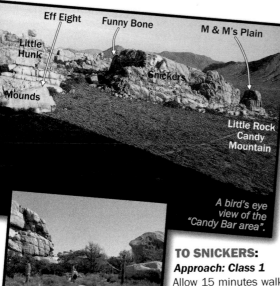

Eff Eight Funny Bone M & M's Plain

Little Hunk

Mounds

Snickers

Little Rock Candy Mountain

A bird's eye view of the "Candy Bar area".

A bird's eye view (well, actually a view from the top of Bambi Meets Godzilla) of the "Candy Bar area". The trail heading off to the lower right of the photo leads you to the Echo Rock parking lot. Eff Eight is on the small formation called Mounds; Funny Bone is on a large formation known as Snickers; and M & M's Plain is on the far side of a separate block called Little Rock Candy Mountain. Is anybody else getting hungry?

A trail leads between Mounds and Snickers (just out of sight on the right).

TO SNICKERS:
Approach: Class 1

Allow 15 minutes walking on trails. Follow the marked trail to the left of the restroom as it leaves the parking area toward Echo Rock. Turn right at a wash and hike around toward the right (east) end of Echo Rock. Circle around the end of Echo Rock to where the trail intersects another trail. Leave these main trails and take a fainter trail to Eff Eight which is the left-slanting crack directly in front of you. As you approach Eff Eight, you'll see a large formation to your right. This is Snickers. The formation on your left is Mounds. Head for a valley between the two large formations.

As the valley narrows, you will intersect a well-defined trail on your right which runs parallel with the Snickers formation into the valley. Follow this trail as it gains ground up a minor hill in front of Snickers.

TO LITTLE ROCK CANDY MOUNTAIN:
Approach: Class 1 (From Parking Area J1)

Allow 15 minutes walking on trails. Follow the marked trail to the left of the restroom as it leaves the parking area toward Echo Rock. Turn right at a wash and hike around toward the right (east) end of Echo Rock. Continue around the end of Echo Rock to where the trail intersects another trail heading to your right. Turn right on this second trail, and follow it to the smaller detached formation at the end of Snickers. This is Little Rock Candy Mountain.

Little Rock Candy Mountain

Echo Rock

Snickers

Little Rock Candy Mountain from the alternate parking.

Circle around to the right of Little Rock Candy Mountain. M & M's Plain is the obvious crack in the middle of the face.

For a more direct approach to M & M's Plain by itself, drive toward Barker Dam for 0.8 miles (1.2 km) from the intersection of Park Boulevard and the Barker Dam Road. Park at the pullout on your left. This pullout is the first one after the turn off to Keys Ranch. Walk east on the road (Parking J2) for approximately 30 yards / meters to the well-defined trail which takes off to your left and heads over toward the climb. Follow the trail until it makes a right turn in a small wash. Leave the trail here and walk to your left over to the base of the route. Allow 10 minutes for this approach.

ROUTE 40

FUN STUFF

DIFFICULTY: 5.8 / 1 pitch

LOCATION:

Echo Rock Area
Echo Cove Parking

SUN / SHADE:

APPROACH: *Class 1*
Allow 5 minutes walking on a trail. Fun Stuff is near the left end of the formation on the left side of the "cove".

EQUIPMENT: Standard Rack.

UPPER BELAY: Belay from the rappel anchor.

DESCENT: *Rappel*
Rappel anchor at top of route.

GENERAL INFORMATION: This is an enjoyable climb with a strenuous start. This route allows for several minor variations. There is one bolt near the start of the route which you may choose to use for protection, as well as a second bolt at an angle to the right above the first bolt. The "standard" route starts about 8 feet to the right but is totally run out. We prefer the bolted variation on lead.

Echo Cove.

ROUTE DESCRIPTION: Friction up the first 10 feet to a minor ledge with a bolt. Traverse up to the right through a broken area toward off-colored flakes. Choose a route through or around the flakes to end up on the right side of the formation. The route finishes with an interesting move at the top of the climb.

ROUTE NOTES:

Date Climbed:　　　　　　Led By:

Climbing Partners:

ECHO ROCK AREA

ROUTE 41

DIFFICULTY: 5.9 / 1 pitch

LOCATION:

Echo Rock Area
Echo Rock Parking

SUN / SHADE:

APPROACH: *Class 2*
Allow 10 minutes easy walking on a good trail, followed by a short scramble. See the approach to **Touch & Go Face.**

EQUIPMENT: Standard Rack.

UPPER BELAY: Create your own.

DESCENT: *Class 3*
There is a convoluted down climb which starts by heading back away from the route to a slot between two rocks. Step across this dicey move and down climb a series of boulders. Turn left and scramble toward the wash through the boulders and bushes until you reach a point that is some 100 feet (30 m) to the left of the start of the route.

GENERAL INFORMATION: If you can climb 5.9, then this route is a must. It's definitely one of the classics in the Park. The route is somewhat deceptive in that it has a series of strenuous moves before you can find a good rest spot. Study the route before you start and get your gear racked accordingly. You don't want to be fumbling around here trying to find the correct piece of protection. You'll earn your bragging rights on this climb. This is a fun, but challenging, route to follow.

Stemming out

ROUTE DESCRIPTION: Start up the crack using a series of stemming moves combined with some solid hand jamming. The first 30 feet (10 m) go pretty straightforward, then you will need to work your way out of the dual crack system up and left to your first real resting spot. More hard work lies ahead. Leave the rest spot and begin a series of strenuous hand and foot jams until you can leave the crack at the top of the route where you will begin a minor traverse to the right. The final few moves above this spot are easier.

ROUTE NOTES:

Date Climbed: _____ Led By: _____

Climbing Partners: _____

ECHO ROCK AREA

ROUTE 42

POPE'S CRACK

DIFFICULTY: 5.9 / 1 pitch

SUN / SHADE:

LOCATION: J1

Echo Rock Area
Echo Rock Parking

APPROACH: *Class 2*
Allow 10 minutes walking on good trails followed by a short scramble. See the approach for **Echo Rock (Pope's Crack)**.

EQUIPMENT: Pro to 3".

UPPER BELAY: Create your own.

DESCENT: *Rappel*
From the top of the route, walk around to the right above a large boulder and ease your way back down to a set of rappel chains located at the same level as the top of the main crack.

GENERAL INFORMATION: This is one of those climbs where speed and technique definitely rule over strength. Your stemming technique had better be at its best or you will wear yourself out attempting to stay on the route with those hand jams. Definitely harder than it looks!

ROUTE DESCRIPTION: The initial stemming moves of the route lull you into a false sense of security; after all, this is a 5.9 climb! About 1/3 of the way up the main crack, you'll find a "thank God ledge" where you can catch your breath. You may never want to leave this spot! Another series of stems, hand-jams, and cursing brings you to the end of the most difficult climbing. Traverse left across the face on a thin ledge, and follow the next crack straight up to the end of the route.

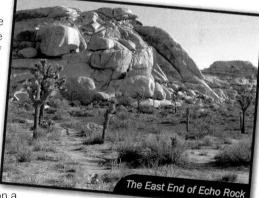
The East End of Echo Rock

ROUTE NOTES:

Date Climbed: Led By:

Climbing Partners:

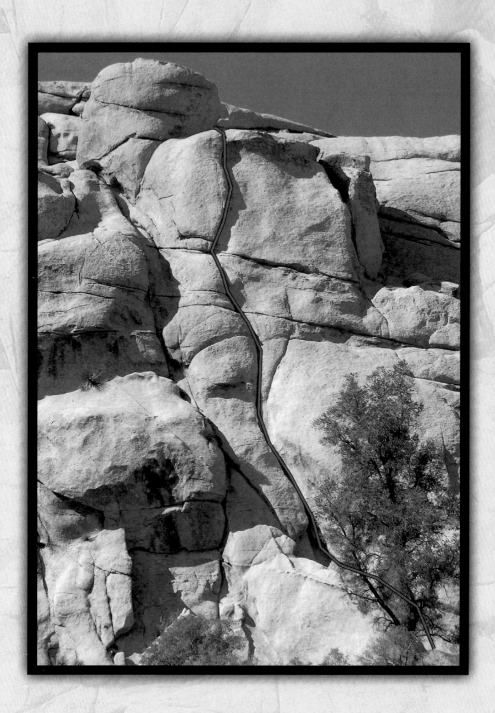

ROUTE 43

BAMBI MEETS GODZILLA

DIFFICULTY: 5.8+ / 1 pitch

LOCATION: J1

Echo Rock Area
Echo Rock Parking

SUN / SHADE:

AM — PM — ASPECT **NE**

APPROACH: *Class 1*
Allow 15 minutes walking on trails. See the approach to **Echo Rock (Bambi Meets Godzilla)**. The route begins directly behind the tall evergreen tree at the base of the formation. There is a deep off-width crack at the start of the climb.

EQUIPMENT: Pro to 3.5".

UPPER BELAY:
Create your own.

DESCENT: *Class 3*
Down climb back away from and then off to your right as you face the route. Follow a down sloping ramp to a tree. Continue past the tree to a point where you can begin to down climb and scramble through the boulders keeping left as you work your way back to the ground.

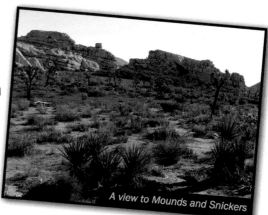

A view to Mounds and Snickers

GENERAL INFORMATION: We always refer to this route as "Bambi Does Godzilla." The real name of the route is probably derived from the classic, 3-minute movie of the same name, Bambi Meets Godzilla, and the results aren't pretty. Maybe Bambi Does Godzilla had a happier ending?

Other routes in this area: Pope's Crack (5.9), Funny Bone (5.8), M & M's Plain (5.9), Eff Eight (5.8).

ROUTE DESCRIPTION: Make your way up past the big block on your left. Start up the off-width crack and follow it as it climbs up the face to a more reasonably sized crack. The difficulty increases as you approach the finish of the climb.

ROUTE NOTES:

Date Climbed:	Led By:
Climbing Partners:	

ECHO ROCK AREA

ROUTE 44

EFF EIGHT

DIFFICULTY: 5.8 / 1 pitch

LOCATION: J2

Echo Rock Area
Echo Rock Parking

SUN / SHADE:

APPROACH: *Class 1*
Allow 15 minutes walking on trails. See the approach to **Mounds**.

EQUIPMENT:
Standard Rack.

UPPER BELAY:
Create your own.

DESCENT: *Class 2*
Down climb by contouring around to the left of the formation and follow it back down to the ground.

GENERAL INFORMATION:
Other routes in this area: Pope's Crack (5.9), M&M's Plain (5.9), Funny Bone (5.8).

ROUTE DESCRIPTION:
Jam your way up the solitary, left-leaning crack.

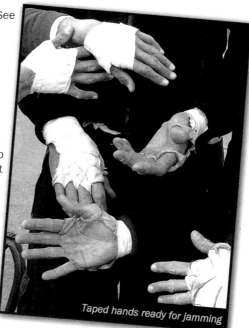
Taped hands ready for jamming

ECHO ROCK AREA

ROUTE NOTES:

Date Climbed:	Led By:
Climbing Partners:	

ROUTE 45

FUNNY BONE

DIFFICULTY: 5.8 / 1 pitch

LOCATION: J1

Echo Rock Area
Echo Rock Parking

SUN / SHADE:

AM	PM	ASPECT
■	■	N

APPROACH: *Class 1*

Allow 15 minutes walking on trails. See the approach to **Snickers**. Head into the valley between the two large formations, **Snickers** and **Little Hunk** (which lies behind **Mounds**).

Shortly you will intersect a well-defined trail on your right which runs parallel with the **Snickers** formation. Follow this trail as it gains ground up a minor hill. Look at the wall on your right where you will see a large left leaning crack. The route starts approximately 60 feet (18m) left of that crack at the highest point of the hill, and to the left of the two large boulders that are seen on the skyline. This point is approximately 10 feet (3 m) to the right of a huge yucca at the base of the wall.

EQUIPMENT: Standard Rack.

UPPER BELAY: Rappel Anchor.

DESCENT: *Rappel*

Rappel anchor just right of the top of the route on a big block.

GENERAL INFORMATION: This is a route that looks harder than it is. There are a couple of nice rest spots along the route. The moves include everything from jamming to stemming to some fun face climbing. Don't miss this one!

Other routes in this area: Eff Eight (5.8), Pope's Crack (5.9), M & M's Plain (5.9) and Bambi Meets Godzilla (5.8+).

High on Funny Bone

ROUTE DESCRIPTION: Start up the route by climbing up through a slightly broken section up to the first small ledge. From here the route heads up to another ledge and then off slightly right to the final crack which leads up to the final moves. At this point move to the right below a big block to a belay spot.

ROUTE NOTES:

Date Climbed:	Led By:
Climbing Partners:	

ECHO ROCK AREA

ROUTE 46

M & M'S PLAIN

DIFFICULTY: 5.9 / 1 pitch

SUN / SHADE:

LOCATION:

Echo Rock Area
Echo Rock Parking or Alternative Parking.

APPROACH: *Class 1*
Allow 15 minutes walking on trails. See the approach to **Little Rock Candy Mountain**.

EQUIPMENT: Standard Rack.

UPPER BELAY:
Belay from the rappel anchor.

DESCENT: *Rappel*
Rappel anchor at top of route.

GENERAL INFORMATION:
This route is enjoyable in the afternoon when some of the other routes are getting too much sun. The flaring crack can be challenging to protect. Also a good route to climb on weekends when Lost Horse and Real Hidden Valley are very busy.

View from M & M's Plain

Other routes in this area: Pope's Crack (5.9), Funny Bone (5.8), Bambi Meets Godzilla (5.8+), Eff Eight (5.8)

ROUTE DESCRIPTION: Follow this vertical crack to the top. The crux is about halfway up the route in the form of an awkward move, which is just out of reach for shorter folks.

ROUTE NOTES:

Date Climbed:	Led By:
Climbing Partners:	

ECHO ROCK AREA

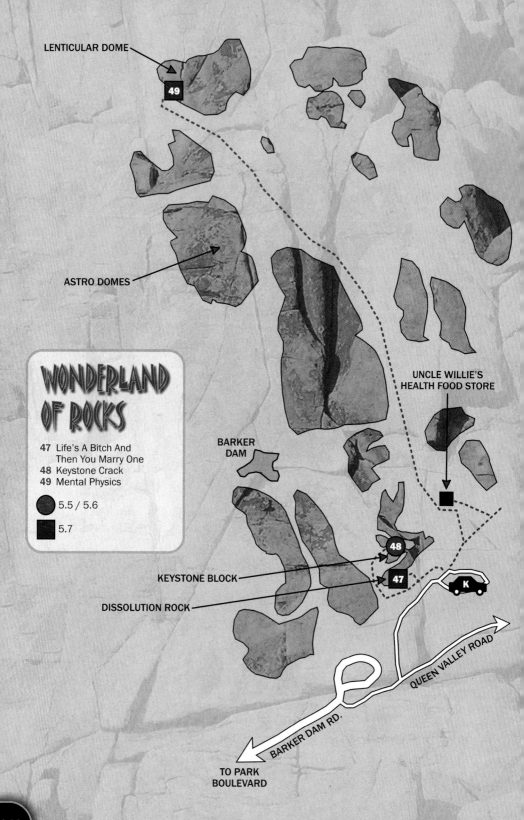

LENTICULAR DOME

49

ASTRO DOMES

WONDERLAND OF ROCKS

47 Life's A Bitch And
   Then You Marry One
48 Keystone Crack
49 Mental Physics

⬤ 5.5 / 5.6
◼ 5.7

BARKER
DAM

UNCLE WILLIE'S
HEALTH FOOD STORE

◼

48

KEYSTONE BLOCK

47

K

DISSOLUTION ROCK

QUEEN VALLEY ROAD

BARKER DAM RD.

TO PARK
BOULEVARD

WONDERLAND OF ROCKS AREA – ACCESS

PARKING:

FORMATIONS: Dissolution Rock (for Route **47** Life's a Bitch and Then You Marry One)
Keystone Block (for Route **48** Keystone Crack)
Lenticular Dome (for Route **49** Mental Physics)

LOCATION: From the intersection of Park Boulevard and Barker Dam Road, drive 1.5 miles (2.4 km) on Barker Dam Road to the entrance of the Barker Dam Parking lot. Instead of entering the lot, turn right onto the dirt Queen Valley Road. Drive 0.1 mile (0.2 km) along the dirt Queen Valley Road to the first left turn. Turn left here and proceed for 0.2 mile (0.3 km) to a small parking lot.

Hunk Rock   Dissolution Rock   Keystone Block

Dissolution Rock seen from the parking area.

TO DISSOLUTION ROCK:
Approach: Class 2
Allow 10 minutes of walking along a trail followed by an easy scramble. Follow the Barker Dam Loop trail that starts from the parking area and curves left toward Dissolution Rock. Leave the trail when you reach a spot below the formation. A short scramble takes you up to the base of the climb.

TO KEYSTONE BLOCK:

Approach: Class 2

Allow 10 minutes of walking along sometimes faint trails followed by an easy scramble. Follow the Barker Dam Loop trail as it leaves the parking area, curves left, and heads parallel to the dirt road. Follow this trail as it winds its way over to the corridor between **Dissolution Rock** and **Hunk Rock**. This area can be identified by the signs prohibiting climbing/bouldering in the area containing petroglyphs, which is directly behind these signs.

Turn right at the signs and hike up the faint trail between the formations until you are on the backside of **Dissolution Rock**, which will be on your right. Continue hiking to the end of a huge, flat rock, then walk another 20 feet (6 m) along a trail. Turn right and scramble on boulders to get around a huge yucca and a tree blocking a corridor.

The approach to **Keystone Block**.

The trail to **Dissolution Rock** and **Keystone Block** starts next to the sign on the extreme left side of the photo.

The long hike to **Lenticular Dome** starts off on the wide "Wall Street Mill Trail" seen leaving the parking area on the right side of this view.

TO LENTICULAR DOME:

Approach: Class 2

Allow 1 hour of cross-country walking across the desert followed by a short scramble. Begin walking along the wide "Wall Street Mill Trail" that starts to the left of the restroom. After walking about 100 yards, take the left fork of the trail. Shortly, you'll come to Uncle Willie's Health Food Store - closed for the season! In fact, Uncle Willie's has been closed for many seasons.

Uncle Willie's Health Food Store

The Astro Domes dominate the landscape.

Turn left just before reaching the building ruins, and walk to the main wash. Turn right, and head "upstream" past an old dam. Continue following the main wash. After walking for about 15 - 20 minutes, you'll come to a more open area. Two very prominent formations will be to your left - **South** and **North Astro Domes**.

Once you reach a point directly in front of the **Astro Domes**, you'll be able to spot your destination ahead of you: **Lenticular Dome**, with its dark colored face and very visible series of vertical cracks.

There are numerous small washes through this open area. Stay generally to the left of the "valley", still following a prominent wash. As you get close to **Lenticular Dome**, the wash will be blocked by boulders.

Lenticular Dome

Lenticular Dome can be spotted ahead once you reach a point near Astro Domes.

Scramble around the obstacles, and drop back into the sandy wash. Within a few steps on flat ground, you will encounter a distinct trail leaving the wash to your right. Follow this trail uphill, then climb up, among, over, and under a maze of boulders, making your way to a rock platform in front of the face of the dome.

WONDERLAND OF ROCKS

ROUTE `47`

LiFE'S A BiTCH AND THEN YOU MARRY ONE

DIFFICULTY: 5.7 / 1 pitch

LOCATION: K

Wonderland of Rocks
Wall Street Mill Parking

SUN / SHADE:

AM	PM	ASPECT
		NE

APPROACH: *Class 2*
Allow 5 minutes of walking along a trail followed by an easy scramble. See the approach to **Dissolution Rock**.

Scramble up a few boulders to the start of the route which is on the dark colored formation up and to your right as you were walking along the trail parallel to the road.

EQUIPMENT: Standard Rack.

UPPER BELAY: Create your own.

DESCENT: *Rappel*
Rappel anchor to the right of the route.

GENERAL INFORMATION: This is a short, fun, steep hand crack that will get your head on for some more serious climbing later in the day. Its short approach makes it a perfect route to begin or end your climbing day. Other routes in the area: Keystone Crack (5.6).

ROUTE DESCRIPTION: Start climbing at a large boulder split by a crack or scramble up right to a ledge at the base of the steeper climbing.

A couple of easier moves bring you up to the short steeper middle section of the route. About the time you think it's harder than you expected, the moves get easier. This route has good opportunities for placing protection.

ROUTE NOTES:

Date Climbed:	Led By:
Climbing Partners:	

WONDERLAND OF ROCKS

ROUTE 48

KEYSTONE CRACK

DIFFICULTY: 5.6 / 1 pitch

LOCATION:

Wonderland of Rocks
Wall Street Mill Parking

SUN / SHADE:

APPROACH: *Class 2*
Allow 10 minutes of walking along a faint trail followed by an easy scramble. See the approach to **Keystone Block**.

Scramble up into a corridor with **Keystone Block** forming its right wall. The start of the route is on the left end of the face, near the top of the corridor.

EQUIPMENT: Standard Rack.

UPPER BELAY: Create your own.

DESCENT: *Class 3*
Scramble down to the left as you face the route then back toward the face of the climb down through the boulders.

GENERAL INFORMATION:
An interesting left-slanting diagonal crack exists 10 feet (3 m) to the right of Keystone Crack. This route may present more of a challenge than Keystone Crack. Other routes in the area: Life's a Bitch and Then You Marry One (5.7).

Cholla cacti

ROUTE DESCRIPTION: Climb the slightly "S" curving crack on the left side of the face. Halfway up the wall, take the left crack.

ROUTE NOTES:

Date Climbed: Led By:

Climbing Partners:

WONDERLAND OF ROCKS

ROUTE 49

MENTAL PHYSICS

DIFFICULTY: 5.7+ / 1 pitch

LOCATION:

Wonderland of Rocks
Wall Street Mill Parking

SUN / SHADE:

APPROACH: *Class 2*

Allow 1 hour of cross-country walking on trails and in washes, followed by a short scramble. See the approach to **Lenticular Dome**.

Pay attention to where you are going and where you have been, as you don't want to get lost in this area which we commonly refer to as the "Wanderland of Rocks". A hiker was lost without food or water in this area for four days in the spring of 2003.

EQUIPMENT: 2 ropes for rappel.

UPPER BELAY: Belay from chains at the top of the crack.

DESCENT: *Rappel (requires 2 ropes)*
Rappel from chains at top of route.

GENERAL INFORMATION: This is another of those "must do" routes and one that many climbers include on their "tick list" for their first visit to the Park.

Although a 2nd pitch is possible, the upper portion of this route isn't very aesthetic. We suggest you savor the outstanding 1st pitch and call it a "done deal".

ROUTE DESCRIPTION: The route begins down among some boulders, and offers easy face climbing at the start. As you get higher in the crack, abundant

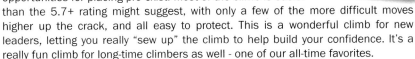
Approaching Mental Physics

opportunities for placing pro exist. Most of the climb is easier than the 5.7+ rating might suggest, with only a few of the more difficult moves higher up the crack, and all easy to protect. This is a wonderful climb for new leaders, letting you really "sew up" the climb to help build your confidence. It's a really fun climb for long-time climbers as well - one of our all-time favorites.

ROUTE NOTES:

Date Climbed: Led By:

Climbing Partners:

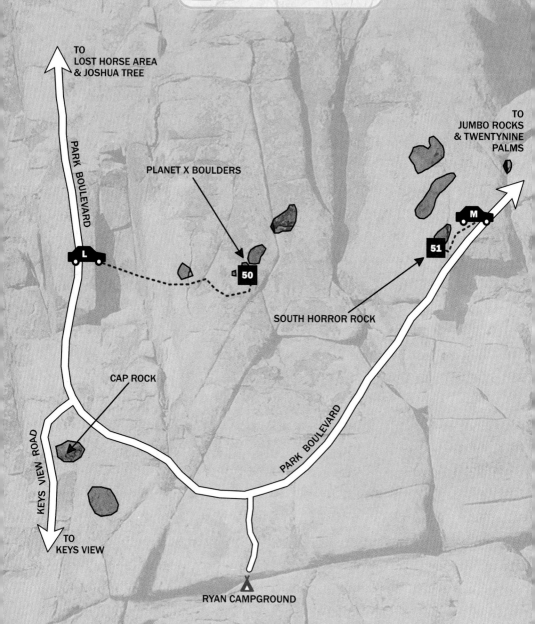

SHEEP PASS AREA - ACCESS

PARKING:

FORMATIONS: Planet X Boulders (for Route **50** Planet X)

LOCATION: From the intersection of Park Boulevard and Keys View Road, drive 0.3 mile (0.5 km) toward Hidden Valley. Park at the first pull-out on the right.

Alternately, from the intersection of Park Boulevard and Barker Dam Road, drive 1.2 miles (1.9 km) toward Keys View Road. Park in the pull-out on the left side of the road.

TO PLANET X BOULDERS:
Approach: Class 1

Allow 15 minutes of easy walking on a faint trail. Look from your parking area east toward the huge Saddle Rock formation in the far distance. Follow a faint climber trail with Access Fund markers in the general direction of Saddle Rock. Follow this trail as it proceeds to a group of boulders, swinging around to the right of them to a second set of rocks. Walk to the right again at the second group. Planet X is on the east side of the tallest rock in the second group.

Saddle Rock

*The isolated **Planet X Boulders** are lost in the foreground between the parking area and the huge Saddle Rock formation.*

PARKING:

FORMATIONS: South Horror Rock (for Route **51** Lazy Day).

LOCATION: Parking for this climb is located in the paved parking lot (the Hall of Horrors lot) across the road from the huge Saddle Rock formation.

From the intersection of Park Boulevard and Keys View Road, drive east for 1.4 miles (2.2 km) and turn left into the parking lot. Or, from Ryan Mountain parking lot, drive west for 0.5 miles (0.8 km) and turn right. This route is located almost directly across the road from Saddle Rock, on the same side of the road as the parking lot.

TO SOUTH HORROR ROCK:
Approach: Class 1

Allow 5 minutes for a walk from the parking area to the base of the route.

South Horror Rock

North Horror Rock

Lazy Day

***Lazy Day** is on the far left side of **South Horror Rock**.*

ROUTE 50

PLANET X

DIFFICULTY: 5.8+ / 1 pitch

LOCATION:

Sheep Pass Area
Planet X Parking

SUN / SHADE:

APPROACH: *Class 1*
Allow 15 minutes of easy walking on a faint trail. See the approach to **Planet X Boulders.**

EQUIPMENT: Standard Rack.

BELAY: Create your own.

DESCENT: *Rappel*
Rappel anchor at top of formation, to the left of Planet X, above the Planet Y climb.

Planet X cactus start

GENERAL INFORMATION: This route is a little off the beaten path but is a fun climb. We try to do it every time we're in the Park. You're unlikely to find other climbers there so it can be a good alternative climb when other routes are busy.

ROUTE DESCRIPTION: The route starts off with a couple of fun moves which provide solid hands and then moves up to some straightforward enjoyable crack climbing. The crack dies out near the top of the route and you must switch to your friction technique. There is one bolt at the top of the crack and one mean cactus at the bottom of the crack.

ROUTE NOTES:

Date Climbed:	Led By:
Climbing Partners:	

SHEEP PASS AREA

ROUTE 51

LAZY DAY

DIFFICULTY: 5.7 / 1 pitch

LOCATION:
Sheep Pass Area
Hall of Horrors Parking

SUN / SHADE:

APPROACH: *Class 1*
Allow 5 minutes for a walk from the parking area to the base of the route, located near the left end of **South Horror Rock** as viewed from the road.

EQUIPMENT: Standard Rack.

UPPER BELAY: Create your own.

DESCENT: *Class 3*
Climb up from the belay a short distance to a deep crack, then work your way left and begin to down climb diagonally away from the road on slabs until you can reverse your direction and head back toward the start of the climb.

GENERAL INFORMATION: This can be a popular route due to the short nature of its approach. Stop and give it a "go" if you're in the area. The climb itself is short and sweet.

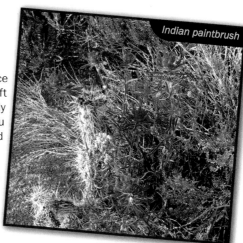
Indian paintbrush

ROUTE DESCRIPTION: Shortly after you start up the route you'll encounter a "dog leg" to the right followed by an awkward vertical move which is probably the crux. Beginning climbers may have a little problem here (as we did) trying to figure out just how to get around this area. The problem works itself out after a few tries and the climbing is straightforward afterwards as it follows the crack to the top.

ROUTE NOTES:

Date Climbed: Led By:

Climbing Partners:

SHEEP PASS AREA

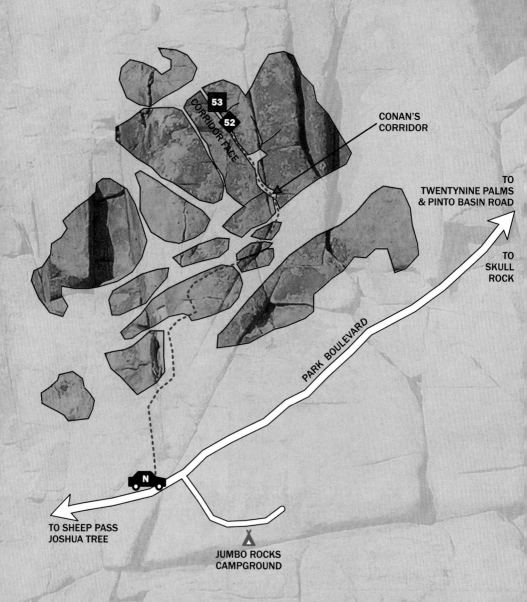

JUMBO ROCKS

52 Colorado Crack
53 Gem

■ 5.8

◆ 5.9

53
52

CORRIDOR FACE

CONAN'S
CORRIDOR

TO
TWENTYNINE PALMS
& PINTO BASIN ROAD

TO
SKULL
ROCK

PARK BOULEVARD

N

TO SHEEP PASS
JOSHUA TREE

JUMBO ROCKS
CAMPGROUND

JUMBO ROCKS - ACCESS

PARKING:

FORMATIONS: Conan's Corridor (for Route ◆52 Colorado Crack, and Route 53 Gem)

LOCATION: Park at the Jumbo Rocks parking area, located across the road from the entrance to Jumbo Rocks Campground.

Turn right in front of this formation

TO CONAN'S CORRIDOR:
Approach: Class 2
Allow 20 minutes of hiking into a maze of rock formations through a very narrow corridor. Leave the parking area and proceed away from the road toward the first large wall you see toward the right. This wall has a dike running vertically down its center. Turn right when you come to this wall and walk along its base until you reach the end of the formation. Turn left here and hike toward another wall with a vertical dike.

Squeeze through Conan's Corridor to reach the climbs.

Scramble down and around a corner to get your first view of Conan's Corridor.

Scramble up to the right onto a lower rock slab and into a small corridor. Follow the corridor for about 50 yards/meters until you see a faint trail heading off to your left. Take this trail over a rock hump and turn right into the next corridor. Proceed along this corridor by scrambling over small boulders and stepping across a few wide spots, staying up off the floor of the corridor on mostly flat boulders. This will lead you to the end of the corridor.

Scramble down off the boulders on the left side of the corridor into the bushes, to a trail which leads to the left toward Conan's Corridor. Once through the long, narrow corridor you will need to scramble up the sloping ramp in front of you. You may be happier if you're wearing shoes with sticky rubber before you head up the ramp.

53
52
The top portion of **Colorado Crack** and **Gem.**

ROUTE 52

DIFFICULTY: 5.9 / 1 pitch

LOCATION:

Jumbo Rocks Area
Jumbo Rocks Parking

SUN / SHADE:

APPROACH: *Class 2*
Allow 20 minutes of hiking through a maze of rock formations followed by a squeeze through a very narrow corridor. See the approach to **Conan's Corridor**.

After squeezing through Conan's Corridor, look to your left to see the **Corridor Face**. Colorado Crack is the prominent crack located about halfway up the face.

EQUIPMENT: 1 - 60m rope or 2 - 50m ropes (One 50m rope will not reach the ground when rappelling). Pro to 3".

UPPER BELAY: Belay from the anchors at the top of the route.

DESCENT: *Rappel or Class 2*
Rappel anchor located at top of route. Note the need for one 60m or two 50m ropes on rappel. You can also descend by heading to the left and working your way back down to the valley where you entered the narrow corridor.

GENERAL INFORMATION: This is one of the more popular climbs in the Park, and, yes, another one of our 10 favorites. It is probably one of the easiest 5.9 climbs you will ever do. This route works well with a double rope system.

If Colorado Crack is already occupied, consider climbing Gem (5.8) located 50 feet (15 m) to the right of Colorado Crack. Since this is called Colorado Crack, we think of its sister as Gem Crack.

ROUTE DESCRIPTION: Follow the crack as it angles right and up to where it narrows and then widens on its way to the top of the route. The lower portion of the route involves some fine hand jams combined with good foot placements on the face. There is a good left hand cling hold located on the right side of the middle section of the crack which can be combined with a wonderful "jug" on the right face above this spot. Hand sequence is important here or you won't be able to easily crank on the right face jug hold.

If you're having a problem toward the top, think chimney moves. Use your feet in behind you. There are excellent protection possibilities on this route.

ROUTE NOTES:

Date Climbed:	Led By:
Climbing Partners:	

JUMBO ROCKS

ROUTE

DIFFICULTY: 5.8 / 1 pitch

LOCATION:

Jumbo Rocks
Jumbo Rocks Parking

SUN / SHADE:

APPROACH: *Class 2*

Allow 20 minutes of hiking through a maze of rock formations followed by a squeeze through a very narrow corridor. See the approach to **Conan's Corridor**.

After squeezing through Conan's Corridor, look to your left to see the **Corridor Face**. Gem is the prominent crack located toward the right end of the wall as you face it.

EQUIPMENT: 1 - 60m rope or 2 - 50m ropes (One 50m rope will not reach the ground when rappelling). Pro to 3".

UPPER BELAY: Create your own.

DESCENT: *Rappel or Class 2*

Rappel back down the face from bolts at the top of Colorado Crack. Note the need for one 60m or two 50m ropes on rappel.

If Colorado Crack is being climbed, continue past the top of Colorado Crack, working your way down and away from the face. Eventually you'll return to "ground level", and can squeeze back through the corridor to return to the base of the route.

GENERAL INFORMATION: This is one of the more popular climbs in the Park, and also one of our 10 favorites. Consider climbing Colorado Crack (5.9) located 50 feet (15 m) to the left of Gem if Gem is occupied.

ROUTE DESCRIPTION: It is possible to girth hitch a sling around a natural feature at the bottom of the route to keep your protection from zippering out in the event of a fall. The lower portion of the route involves some fine hand jams combined with innovative foot placements on the face. The top portion of the route allows you to practice some enjoyable hand/foot jamming crack climbing technique. Probably a good idea to tape up for this one.

Due to the sustained nature of the route, we feel that Gem at 5.8 might actually be a little more difficult than Colorado Crack (5.9)!

ROUTE NOTES:

Date Climbed:	Led By:
Climbing Partners:	

JUMBO ROCKS

SPLIT ROCKS

◆ 5.8

◆ 5.9

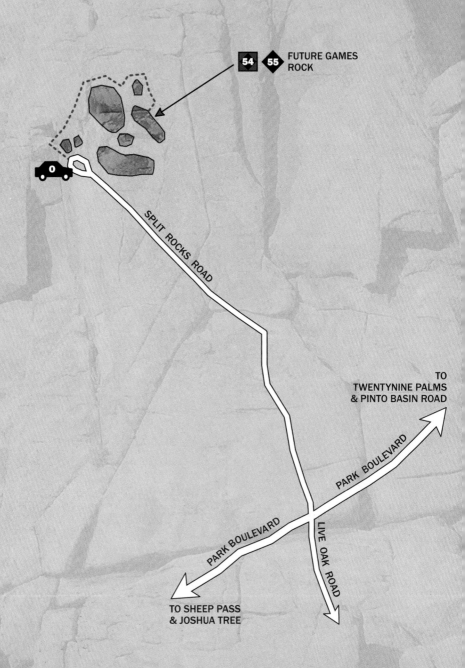

54 **55** FUTURE GAMES ROCK

0

SPLIT ROCKS ROAD

TO
TWENTYNINE PALMS
& PINTO BASIN ROAD

PARK BOULEVARD

PARK BOULEVARD

LIVE OAK ROAD

TO SHEEP PASS
& JOSHUA TREE

SPLIT ROCKS - ACCESS

PARKING:

FORMATIONS: Future Games Rock (for Route **54** Continuum, and Route **55** Invisibility Lessons).

LOCATION: From the intersection of Park Boulevard and Pinto Basin Road, drive 2.2 miles (3.5 km) west on Park Boulevard to the Split Rocks road on your right (Live Oak Road is on your left). Turn right and drive to the Split Rocks parking area.

TO FUTURE GAMES ROCK:

Approach: Class 1

Allow 15 minutes of easy walking on a good trail. Follow the trail as it contours around the left side of a very large split boulder located at the edge of the parking area.

The trail heads down a series of sculpted steps toward a very large boulder. Take a hard right at the boulder toward a tall split rock formation in the distance. If you continue straight instead of turning right, you'll be on a nature trail which takes you away from the climb.

The trail is fairly well marked and generally parallels the formations on your right. Once past the split rock, the climbs are visible on the wall to your right. **Please see page 167 for the routes on Future Games Rock.**

Walk left around the large split rock to find the start of the trail.

Future Games Rock

Future Games Rock lies beyond a tall formation with a dramatic split down its center.

ROUTE 54

CONTINUUM

DIFFICULTY: 5.8+ / 1 pitch

LOCATION:

Split Rocks
Split Rocks Parking

APPROACH: *Class 1*
Allow 15 minutes of easy walking on a good trail. See the approach to **Future Games Rock.**

EQUIPMENT: Pro to 3".

UPPER BELAY: Create your own.

DESCENT: *Class 1*
An exceptionally easy walk-off to your left as you face the route.

GENERAL INFORMATION:
The walk-off makes the route worthwhile if nothing else does. Consider combining this route with Invisibility Lessons (5.9).

SUN / SHADE:

Future Games Rock

ROUTE DESCRIPTION: Start in the left crack and reach a good stance after about 20 feet (6 m) of hard hand jamming. This is probably the crux of the route.

The crack continues up to a point where the route angles right. Some folks find the climbing along this section to be awkward. Follow the crack up to the top of the route.

ROUTE NOTES:

Date Climbed: _____ Led By: _____

Climbing Partners: _____

ROUTE 55

INVISIBILITY LESSONS

DIFFICULTY: 5.9 / 1 pitch

SUN / SHADE:

AM	PM	ASPECT
■	■	N

LOCATION:

Split Rocks
Split Rocks Parking

APPROACH: *Class 1*
Allow 15 minutes of easy walking on a good trail. See the approach to **Future Games Rock.**

EQUIPMENT: Pro to 3".

UPPER BELAY: Create your own.

DESCENT: *Class 1*
An exceptionally easy walk-off to your left as you face the route.

GENERAL INFORMATION: This is one of the "classic" 5.9 routes in this Guide. If you can lead this route plus Touch and Go (5.9) and Pope's Crack (5.9) with impunity (that's no whining), then you can consider yourself a solid 5.9 climber!

Consider combining this route with Continuum (5.8), the right-sloping crack to the left of this climb.

Invisibility Lessons start

ROUTE DESCRIPTION: This route begins with a very delicate finger crack, then transitions into a strenuous hand crack. Look for features on either side of the crack for foot placements. At least, that's what the belayer kept telling us. Higher, the crack widens somewhat; you'll be happy you carried up some larger pro for this section.

ROUTE NOTES:

Date Climbed: Led By:

Climbing Partners:

SPLIT ROCKS

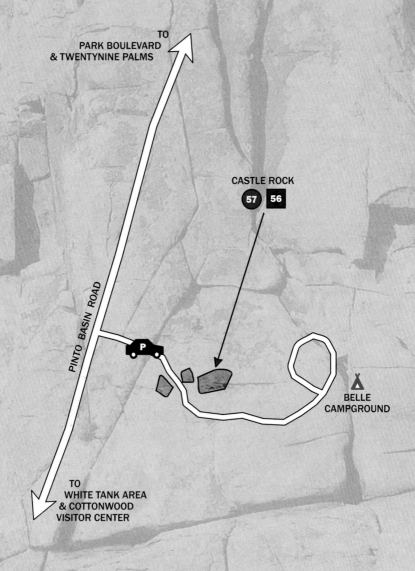

BELLE CAMPGROUND AREA

56 Music Box   **57** Diagnostics

 5.5 / 5.6

■ 5.8

TO
PARK BOULEVARD
& TWENTYNINE PALMS

CASTLE ROCK
57 **56**

PINTO BASIN ROAD

P

BELLE
CAMPGROUND

TO
WHITE TANK AREA
& COTTONWOOD
VISITOR CENTER

BELLE CAMPGROUND - ACCESS

PARKING: 🅿️

FORMATIONS: **Castle Rock** (for Route **56** Music Box, and Route **57** Diagnostics).

LOCATION: Belle Campground/Castle Rock. From the intersection of Park Boulevard and Pinto Basin Road, drive 1.3 miles (2.1 km) south on Pinto Basin Road to Belle Campground. The entrance to the campground is on the left side of the road. Park in a non-campsite parking area near the entrance to the campground.

TO CASTLE ROCK:
Approach: Class 1
A very short approach for this route as the climb is located in the campground. This formation is adjacent to campsite #3, the first campsite you'll encounter on the left side of the road in the Belle Campground. Ask permission to climb from anyone who might be camped in that site. Avoid walking though the campsite as you approach these routes.

*Placing pro on **Diagnostics.***

Music Box

Diagnostics

Downclimb

Castle Rock seen from the campground entrance.

ROUTE 56

MUSIC BOX

DIFFICULTY: 5.8 / 1 pitch

SUN / SHADE:

AM	PM	ASPECT
■	■	N

LOCATION:

Belle Campground
Belle Campground Parking

APPROACH: *Class 1*
Walk a very short distance to this climb located in the campground. This route is approximately 150 feet (72 m) to the left of campsite #3. Avoid walking though the campsite as you approach this route. It is the last significant crack on the left end of the north face.

EQUIPMENT: Pro to 3".

UPPER BELAY: Create your own.

DESCENT: *Class 3*
Down climb the knobby slab located near the right end of the formation.

Tenacious tree

GENERAL INFORMATION: You usually won't see other climbers on this route so it can be a good alternative climb during busy weekends. It's time to "face the music!" Consider combining this route with Diagnostics (5.6), the dihedral to your right.

ROUTE DESCRIPTION: This sometimes off-width crack will test your crack climbing skills. Try not to show fear as you inch your way up through those painful lower jams. What you see is what you get on this climb. It's crack, crack, crack. Although enjoyable in a sick sort of way, this is not one of our friends' favorite routes. But then, they have no class (or why would they be climbing with us?).

ROUTE NOTES:

Date Climbed:	Led By:
Climbing Partners:	

BELLE CAMPGROUND

ROUTE

DIAGNOSTICS

DIFFICULTY: 5.6 / 1 pitch

LOCATION:

Belle Campground
Belle Campground Parking

SUN / SHADE:

APPROACH: *Class 1*
Walk a very short distance to this climb located in the campground. This route is approximately 80 feet (24 m) to the left of campsite #3. Ask permission to climb if anyone is camped at this site. Avoid walking though the campsite as you approach this route. It is the obvious dihedral toward the right end of the north face.

EQUIPMENT: Standard Rack.

UPPER BELAY: Create your own.

DESCENT: *Class 3*
Down climb the knobby slab located to the right of the route.

GENERAL INFORMATION: You usually won't see other climbers on this route so it can be a good alternative climb when other areas get busy. This is a short, fun warm up for the dreaded Music Box (5.8) route located some 50 feet (15 m) to your left.

Diagnostics lie-back

ROUTE DESCRIPTION: This is just one of those strenuous dihedral climbs. No funny stuff here. Make a couple of moves off the ground and get into your hand jamming posture as you work your way up to the top. There are a few features on the face to help you through the lower portion of the route. You can stay in the crack or move out to the face on your right to finish the route.

ROUTE NOTES:

Date Climbed: _____   Led By: _____

Climbing Partners: _____

BELLE CAMPGROUND

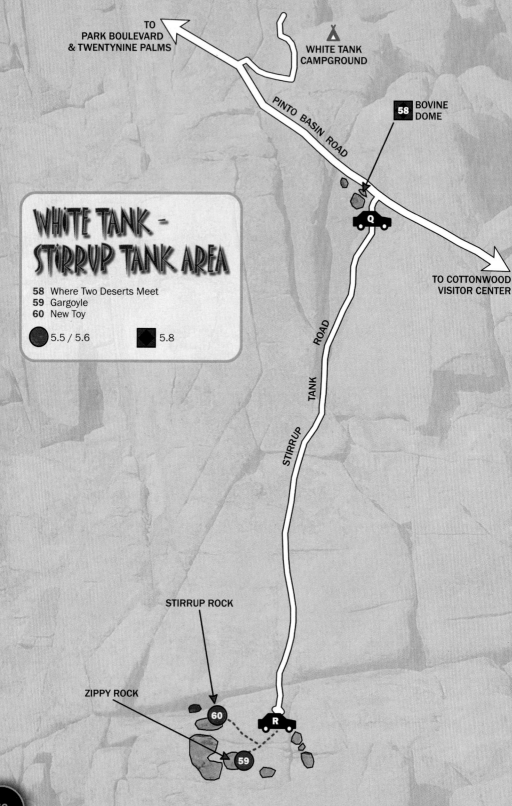

TO
PARK BOULEVARD
& TWENTYNINE PALMS

WHITE TANK
CAMPGROUND

PINTO BASIN ROAD

58 BOVINE
DOME

Q

TO COTTONWOOD
VISITOR CENTER

WHITE TANK –
STIRRUP TANK AREA

58 Where Two Deserts Meet
59 Gargoyle
60 New Toy

⬤ 5.5 / 5.6   ◆ 5.8

STIRRUP TANK ROAD

STIRRUP ROCK

ZIPPY ROCK

60

R

59

WHITE TANK - STIRRUP TANK AREA - ACCESS

PARKING: [Q]

FORMATIONS: Bovine Dome (for Route **58** Where Two Deserts Meet).

LOCATION: Stirrup Tank (near White Tank Campground) / Bovine Dome. From the intersection of Park Boulevard and Pinto Basin Road, drive 3.0 miles (4.8 km) south on Pinto Basin Road toward Cottonwood Visitor Center. Turn right on Stirrup Tank Road and park in the paved parking area next to the intersection.

TO BOVINE DOME:
Approach: Class 1
Leave your vehicle and proceed approximately 100 feet (30 m) straight ahead from the front of your car. This route lies on the end of the formation to your left. (See photo overleaf.)

PARKING: [R]

FORMATIONS: Zippy Rock (for Route **59** Gargoyle).
Stirrup Rock (for Route **60** New Toy).

LOCATION: From the intersection of Park Boulevard and Pinto Basin Road, drive 3.0 miles (4.8 km) south on Pinto Basin Road toward Cottonwood Visitor Center. Turn right on Stirrup Tank Road and drive to the parking area at the end of the dirt road.

TO ZIPPY ROCK:
Approach: Class 1
Allow 5 minutes walking on a faint trail. Leave the parking area and follow the somewhat faint trail which runs in the same direction as the road. Hike over to a wash located near the formation in front of you. **Zippy Rock** is straight ahead, and Gargoyle is the short crack at the left end of the formation.

TO STIRRUP ROCK:
Approach: Class 2
Allow 10 minutes walking on faint trails and in washes, plus a short scramble. Leave the parking area and follow the somewhat faint trail which runs in the same direction as the road. Hike over to a wash located near the formation in front of you.

Turn right at the wash and walk roughly 200 yards / meters toward the end of the next few large formations on your left. Turn left as you pass the end of a large formation which has a long, vertical crack in its center.

You'll see a dramatic crack on Stirrup Rock as you first approach it (see photo on page 179). Don't panic - New Toy is not this 5.10c crack! Continue along the wash, passing to the right of the formation, and circle around to the opposite site of Stirrup Rock.

Follow the trail straight ahead to Gargoyle or turn right to **New Toy**.

Gargoyle

To New Toy

ROUTE **58**

WHERE TWO DESERTS MEET

DIFFICULTY: 5.8 / 1 pitch

SUN / SHADE:

AM PM ASPECT **NW**

LOCATION: Q

White Tank - Stirrup Tank
Pinto Basin Road - Stirrup Tank Road Intersection Parking

APPROACH: *Class 1*
Walk a short distance to the base of this climb. See the approach to **Bovine Dome**.

EQUIPMENT: Standard Rack.

UPPER BELAY: Create your own.

DESCENT: *Class 3*
Walk off on the opposite side of the climb toward a gully. Climb down into the gully, turn right and scramble back to the ground.

GENERAL INFORMATION: This is a short, fun route with a very short approach. It seems easier than its 5.8 rating; perhaps 5.7. Several additional climbs are located at the end of the dirt road near the Stirrup Tank parking area. While in this area, be sure to take a trip south down to Cholla Cactus Garden and Ocotillo Patch. The Ocotillo are best viewed in the spring or after a rain when they are in full bloom.

The Colorado and Mojave Deserts meet in this transition area near **Where Two Deserts Meet.**

Walk past the right side of the larger formation to the start of the climb.

ROUTE DESCRIPTION:
Climb the obvious crack at the end of the formation. A few short moves lead to a nice layback section. From there the angle eases off to the finish to the route.

ROUTE NOTES:

Date Climbed:	Led By:
Climbing Partners:	

WHITE TANK - STIRRUP TANK AREA

ROUTE 59

GARGOYLE

DIFFICULTY: 5.6 / 1 pitch

LOCATION:

White Tank - Stirrup Tank
Stirrup Tank Parking

SUN / SHADE:

  NE

APPROACH: *Class 1*
Allow 5 minutes walking on a faint trail. See the approach to **Zippy Rock**. Gargoyle is the obvious crack that splits the left side of the face.

EQUIPMENT: Pro to 3".

UPPER BELAY: Create your own.

DESCENT: *Class 4*
Climb down a steep section directly behind the route. Some climbers might want an upper belay down this section.

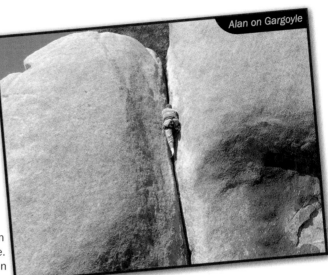

Alan on Gargoyle

GENERAL INFORMATION: This is a short route with a reasonable approach far from the maddening crowd. This is another good area to visit on those busy weekends. Consider combining this route with New Toy (5.6), located just a short distance from the parking area or Where Two Deserts Meet (5.8), located back at the intersection with Pinto Basin Road.

ROUTE DESCRIPTION: Climb the obvious short crack on the left side of the formation. This is a great route to practice your crack climbing technique.

ROUTE NOTES:

Date Climbed:	Led By:
Climbing Partners:	

WHITE TANK - STIRRUP TANK AREA

ROUTE 60

NEW TOY

DIFFICULTY: 5.6 / 1 pitch

LOCATION:

White Tank - Stirrup Tank
Stirrup Tank Parking

SUN / SHADE:

  NW

APPROACH: *Class 2*
Allow 10 minutes walking on faint trails and in washes, plus a short scramble. See the approach to **Stirrup Rock**.

Scramble up some boulders to the start of the route which should be easily visible once you have circled around to the northwest face of the formation.

EQUIPMENT: Pro to 3".

UPPER BELAY:
Create your own.

DESCENT: *Rappel*
Rappel from an anchor located approximately 30 feet (9 m) to your left as you face the route.

GENERAL INFORMATION:
A fun, easier route which does not see much traffic. This is a good route for the beginning climber with plenty of options for placing protection. Consider combining this route with Gargoyle (5.6) or Where Two Deserts Meet (5.8).

Stirrup Rock as you approach it. New Toy is on the opposite side.

ROUTE DESCRIPTION: Start from a stance down between a huge boulder and the face of the main formation. The route follows the obvious curving crack up through an off-width section and then up to the finish.

ROUTE NOTES:

Date Climbed: Led By:

Climbing Partners:

RESOURCES

Alan on Gargoyle

Left-to-Right: Ginni Greer (seated), Gary Hoover, Dave Cooper, Randy Murphy, Diane Winger, Charlie Winger

REFERENCES

Joshua tree

Joshua Tree Rock Climbing Guide
By Randy Vogel
Falcon Books Publisher

Rock Climbs of Central Joshua Tree
Rock Climbs of Lost Horse Valley
Rock Climbs of Hidden Valley
By Alan Bartlett

Mountaineering:The Freedom of the Hills
The Mountaineers Publisher

National Park Service

U.S. Department of the Interior

Joshua Tree National Park

U.S. Geological Survey

U.S. Department of the Interior

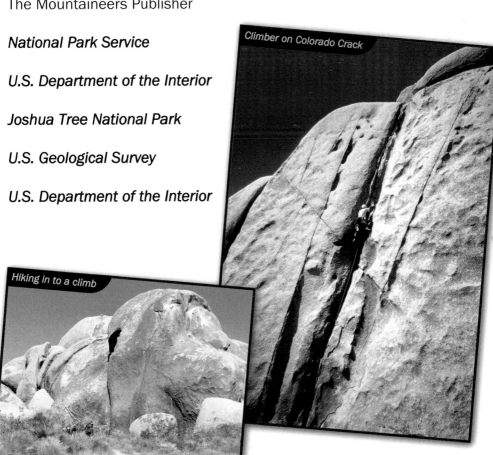
Climber on Colorado Crack

Hiking in to a climb

ABOUT THE AUTHORS

Charlie Winger first visited Joshua Tree along with a group of climbing friends from the Colorado Mountain Club in the late 1980s. After a week-long venture filled with thrills, challenges, defeats, sand-bagging, raw fingertips, stinky climbing shoes, laughs and beer, he was hooked. He returned the following spring, then again with neophyte **Diane** a month later, offering her the dubious thrill of an introduction to friction climbing ("There aren't any holds!" "Sure there are. Put your foot on that shadow there.")

Wingers in Joshua Tree (Randy Murphy)

The bug had struck again. The Wingers began a tradition of scheduling one or two week J-Tree trips every spring; they then discovered the joys of climbing in the fall, and even tossed in some trips between. They like to stay in shape for their Joshua Tree trips by climbing local crags in their native Colorado.

Charlie is a prolific mountaineer who has climbed hundreds of peaks in Colorado (including the 200 highest peaks in the state), California (over 100 Sierra Peaks), the 99 peaks on the Sierra Club's Desert Peaks List, 5 of the 7 (continental) summits, the highpoints of all 50 states, the highpoints of all 64 counties in Colorado, and many more.

Diane takes a more relaxed approach to hiking, with some of her favorite memories being of treks in New Zealand (Milford Track Kepler Track), Peru (Inca Trail to Machu Picchu), and Nepal (Khumbu region/Gokyo Ri), and the local bathrooms after eating at a local street vendor's stand in Amecameca, Mexico.

Charlie and Diane are also the authors of *Highpoints Adventures - The Complete Guide to the 50 State Highpoints* and *The Essential Guide to Great Sand Dunes National Park & Preserve*. They love being out-doors, and love writing about the places they've been. The Wingers moved from Denver to southern Colorado several years ago, and live in a rural area near Beulah.

Charlie leading Count on Your Fingers

INDEX

BY FORMATION